For Dad. The bravest man I know.

Contents

Preface

However ordinary, normal, unremarkable, without training or uneducated in spiritual matters you may think you are, you can change and self-heal without needing to defer to others, or rely on an 'authority' for guidance. You can work on yourself, illuminate your gifts and rediscover a more purposeful life, as you strengthen your connection to the natural world and walk your life path more authentically. Everyone has a right to their own beliefs. Therefore there should be eight billion religions on this planet: eight billion spiritual beliefs. Reading through and working with some of the exercises in this book will hopefully unearth a clearer idea of your spiritual side and help you understand life more deeply, perhaps seeing your place in the world from a new perspective.

In writing this book, I hope to show that we are intrinsically part of the natural world, linked throughout time by our ancestral lineage and the energies that pervade the planet. Those who have lived in connection with the Earth had a wisdom of their own, one that is still pertinent today and helpful to anyone on their journey through life, whether spiritual or not.

Shamanism has become popular in recent years. However, its contemporary form differs from that practised by indigenous nature-connected cultures by being suitable to current, more urbanised, environments. My use of the word 'shamanism' can loosely be interpreted as nature-based spirituality encompassing teachings and wisdom passed down the generations, mixed with spiritual practices adapted for the modern world.

With the compendium of exercises and ideas presented, I am sharing some of the ancient wisdom I have been privileged to be taught, along with my own commentary around philosophy, psychology and how science and spirituality are entwined, often with the boundaries blurred.

This book has been written as a workbook of self-discovery, with tools and techniques to guide you on your spiritual journey. The exercises and practices can also clear emotional or psychological blocks, help you reconnect to the natural world and better understand your place within it.

Although this is an introduction to contemporary shamanism and draws upon earth-connected wisdom, this is not a teach-yourself shamanism book. The best way to learn about this ancient practice is from direct teaching, as it is the shamanic teacher's experience and lineage that are the gateway to authentic understanding.

There are many contemporary shamanic practitioners around the globe offering healing and, if qualified, teaching shamanism in a modern way, sharing their knowledge with those willing to learn. But there are also many opportunities and activities available to the spiritual explorer that embrace our connection to nature, community and ceremony. These include meditation groups, drumming circles, spiritual retreats and mind, body and soul festivals, not to mention the wide range of online resources exploring shamanism and spirituality in general.

Everyone has a right to know about the ancient knowledge and wisdom at the core of shamanism and nature-based spirituality, used for millennia to help people and communities across the planet. That said, I have endeavoured not to reveal any of the practices that should only be passed on through direct teaching. These include some that could be thought of as more sacred or powerful, as they do not translate easily into word form and require the guidance of a qualified shamanic practitioner to be taught effectively. Also, please bear in mind that as the exercises presented are wide-ranging and drawn from various areas, there are likely to be similarities with more traditional processes, even those conducted within a religious framework. Any resemblance is coincidental and not meant to be copying, appropriating or disrespectful.

Please note that the written exercises are suggested for people drawn to writing. For many, writing does not come naturally, so as an alternative, either record your answers and insights on your phone or just think and contemplate upon each exercise, maybe spending time in nature as you do so. Shamanism has, after all, been effective for thousands of years without the written word.

Goal

Your soul (or perhaps, more accurately, your soul purpose) can be thought of as a beautiful gem hidden within you, metaphorically buried in the earth that is you. It has always been there, waiting for you to unearth and reconnect to it. Maybe it has been buried deeply, covered in soil, sand and stone. Buried so far down into the earth that it needs dynamite to blast away the rock, then a mechanical excavator to remove the following few layers, before finally digging with a shovel or hand tool to unearth it. For some, this precious gem may be near the surface and easily dug out with a trowel, but it still requires cleaning with a brush to begin to see its radiance. For those with the gem already in their possession, a final buffing or polish with the softest of cloths will make it sparkle like no other jewel and become the beacon it was meant to be.

This analogy appeals to me, having worked in the manufacturing and engineering industries for twenty-five years; marrying the ethereal soul to the search, mining and final polishing of a gemstone. Engineering meets spirituality, and the process of choosing the right tools for the job. You don't use a sledgehammer to crack a nut, as they say. So the exercises in this book vary in strength or potency – some explosive, bringing instantaneous results and insight, others more subtle and perhaps more applicable to the polishing stage. The distinction will only become apparent when you try them. If some exercises seem pointless or do not resonate, that is fine; please move on until they do seem appropriate. It is, of course, a waste of time trying to dig down fifty metres with a teaspoon.

Introduction

"You have to let it all go Neo. Fear, doubt, disbelief.
Free your mind."
Morpheus, The Matrix.

What shapes us? What moulds us into the person we are? The major factors are our biology and inherited chemistry, our upbringing, the knowledge taught to us and what we have learnt from the world around us. This learning begins with inputs via our senses, translated into information that builds up this picture of who we are. But how much of this information is accurate and what filters has it gone through before it reaches us? Access to information is at an all-time high. We can search for information on any subject under the sun (or beyond the sun, for that matter), where data, as a cascade of inputs, is presented as information, before being rearranged into knowledge, translated into understanding and shared as wisdom. But has this data, knowledge or wisdom been manipulated? How do we know?

It begins with trust. Trusting the source or author of the information and trusting that it is accurate and truthful. In fact, life begins with trust. A newborn is totally at the mercy of the world, and it is the parent's (or guardian's) role and responsibility to look after that infant. The child trusts the parent implicitly. As the child grows, that trust is often extended to all the people the child meets, where the feeling received (or perceived) from the parent is that this new person is a friend, not a foe. A child naturally trusts and learns to defer to an adult, accepting innocently what they say and do.

Arguably, the most significant factor influencing the child is the environment in which it is raised. From the general geography and climate of the area the child has been born into, along with the local and national cultural influences, to specifically the child's family and social and economic level. As St. Ignatius Loyola (some sources cite Aristotle) said, *"Give me a child until he is seven, and I will show you the man."*

Parents want what is best for their children. To keep them safe and, understandably, wish to give them more than they had when they were young, especially when it comes to opportunities in life. But how much of what parents were taught do they pass on to their children? Probably quite a lot. Which, again, is only natural. This is a founding principle of life and, at the most basic level, animal survival – parents pass on what they have been taught to their offspring. Some common expressions popular in England, relating to the natural inheritance of characteristics include, "If it was good enough for me, then it's good enough for you", often said by a parent to a child, and, "Like father, like son", or, "You sound just like your mother!" No doubt, we have all picked up on such expressions when we were young and now, in adulthood, use them with our own children (if we have them) as a form of perceived wisdom.

Unfortunately, not only is the good passed on, but also the not-so-good. From the seemingly innocuous finger-wagging, high-expectation goal setting and the unconscious sharing of bad habits, to being ignored, neglected or even abandoned, not to mention the potentially life-shattering verbal abuse, beating or molestation of a child.

Our worlds as children are shaped by the influencers in our lives, and we trust adults to teach us the right way to live. As children, we naturally adopt parental mannerisms, characteristics and, quite often, their religious or spiritual beliefs. There is no choice as a child.

Furthermore, the home life we are brought up in defines what is the norm for us. How often has it been said by a child that they thought this was normal, especially when referring to some negative behaviour or lifestyle when growing up? If a child had to walk an hour to school, they would think this normal. If they went to church every Sunday, they believed this also to be normal. If they got whipped with their father's belt when they did something wrong, they would grow up thinking this too, was how all children were raised. And sadly, in this last case, as an adult, the patterns of behaviour may continue as parents often behave in a similar way with their own offspring.

Then, at school, the child comes across new rules and systems as the educational establishments impose filters and biases based upon their specific institutional standards, and their take on the correct curriculum to teach. Do modern schools produce rounded, well-educated, independent students? How much of current schooling still harks back to the Victorian mindset of controlling, dominating and indoctrinating children to become followers of the system and churning out obedient workers and, in the modern era, obedient consumers too? The answers to these questions are debatable but perhaps shed light on the lengths (and the cost) some families will go to to ensure their child's acceptance at a particular school.

There is also the issue of gender and the biases boys and girls are treated with. Traditional gender stereotypes are often reinforced by parental, school and cultural behaviours. Gender fluidity is a relatively new concept, but undoubtedly has always been there, even if swept under the carpet by parents or authority figures out of fear, lack of understanding or prejudice. A boy raised to play sports and compete, to be interested in male-centric pastimes and not to show his emotions will become a certain type of man. One raised with love, compassion, encouraged to share his feelings, accept himself and not feel overly pressured will become another sort of man. It is similar for girls. Being dressed in a pink frock, given dolls to play with and helping mum with the cooking are memories that many British women (and undoubtedly other nations' women) probably have, all reinforcing the female gender roles of having to look a certain way and learn about motherhood and housekeeping. There are, of course, biological differences with hormones and body chemistry to consider, but stereotype reinforcement and parenting styles significantly affect a child's development.

So, in our Western societies, children are products of their environments, with little space to explore beyond the influences described above and no clear way to gauge the extent of any dysfunctional upbringing or where their trust may have been misplaced. It is only later in life when the child or, more likely, the young adult starts to question life for his or herself, that they look towards understanding their identity, challenge society's ideas and behaviours, and seek to find their own place in the world. However, does a teenager have the skill set necessary to make informed choices regarding all the information taught, shared, or sought out? Perhaps most notably, in the case of information from the internet, where a considerable amount of filtration, bias and opinion can distort the supposed facts searched for with a few taps on a keypad or a brief voice command.

We are the first generations with information at our fingertips (literally, in the form of smartphones), available almost instantly wherever we are in the world, via the web. This information abundance has now been capitalised upon by corporations as, based on our internet click habits and viewing patterns, they tailor feed to give us more of what they think we want, predominately to make money rather than any form of expansive education. Online we can discover people who think the same, look the same, and seemingly have similar ideas, desires and goals as ourselves. Our online tribe. Within this tribe, some will come across (or even promote themselves) as being successful, exuding a confidence online that is, not surprisingly, very attractive, especially to a younger mind. This could lead to the child or adolescent wishing to emulate or even idolise such an online 'influencer', even though such behaviour can be at odds with living a happy and healthy life. For example, in the case of online fashion influencers, teenage followers want to look like them or follow their so-called beauty advice, often with unachievable expectations. For the more easily influenced individuals, such unfulfilled expectations can lead to depression or, in extreme cases, suicidal thoughts or actions.

Additionally, as soon as we have an online presence (almost a given for any teenager or adolescent), we are open to having our seemingly innocuous posts, photos and videos commented upon and possibly criticised by others and, in extreme cases, even attract abuse and threats. Such online trolling can only negatively impact the psyche, especially that of the young, creating doubts and fears in areas of behaviour where such feelings are in no way justified.

But we want children to experience freedom, not be worried or concerned about every action they take, online or in the real world. We want them to play and have fun, mix with others, learn and grow. But, due to possible exposure to negatively perceived experiences and potentially hazardous situations, rules have been imposed for their safety. Rules around where to play, who to play with, what to eat, what to touch, who to talk to, etc.. To always be safe – safe at school, safe online, safe crossing the road, safe at night and so on. We are removing children's ability to trust and have faith in themselves by building this layer of protection around them: this shield of rules. Children today seem far more enclosed, kept "safe" and mix less with others (physically) than children from previous generations.

What has happened to the days of yore when, to a child, the whole world was seemingly a playground filled with riotous, free-roaming summers, building castles on the beach, playing tag in the cul-de-sac, creating a den in the thicket, exploring the woods, climbing a tree, cawing like a crow or pretending to be a squirrel? Such unfettered play is clearly outside and in nature, often where the limits of safety are pushed, sometimes even overstretched, with tumbles, grazed knees, getting lost or belly aches from scrumping fruit are part of the adventure. Such natural pushing of the boundaries is, more importantly, full of memorable learning and growing experiences.

Jay Griffiths expands on 'The Riddle of the Childscape', as she phrases it, in her wonderfully resonating and heartfelt book *Kith*[1]:

> "Children like thinking and want to learn, but not to be taught a hidden curriculum of hierarchy and obedience in schooling which damages their psyche with stress and overwork. In Euro-American societies, children's minds are in pain – they tell us this over and over again in all the languages they know, including the language of silence, spoken so eloquently by the deeply depressed – yet they are denied many of the psyche's helpers: animal companions, rites of passage in the wild world for their mysterious transitions into adulthood; and the secret places of soul privacy to cocoon themselves, to nurture their butterfly psyche."

We have been shaped and manipulated from the day we were born, throughout childhood and adolescence, absorbing information from those we innocently trust and just accepting that what we experienced as children was normal. It is no different for today's children, surrounded by rules and regulations, bombarded by

---

[1] Jay Griffiths, *Kith: The Riddle of the Childscape*, 2014, Penguin books.

conflicting ideas or having to deflect constant criticism on how they look and what they should think.

All in all, it seems pretty tough to be a child in the modern Western world. But is it any easier being an adult? Where do we find peace nowadays? Wherever you live, you do not have to wait long before hearing the sound of construction, passing traffic (on the road and in the air), dogs barking, alarms, power tools, grass cutting or music blaring out. The sounds of nature are being drowned out or, worse, diminished due to habitat loss. Then there is light pollution flooding the night sky, depriving us of one of the most incredible natural sights, the Milky Way streaking overhead. How many of the next generations will ever see it with their own eyes?

So much is changing, from the loss of clear skies, ancient forests and wild places, to the pollution of our lands, the seas and the air we breathe, even the extinction of whole species. It is terribly sad if we stop, step back and look at what has happened since the start of the industrial revolution, only two hundred years ago: perhaps more so in the recent accelerated information age of the past thirty years. The pros of such progress have become almost a given – material goods, fast foods, a constant fuel and energy supply, access to technology that provides virtually instantaneous information, communication and entertainment, and a general acceptance that more is better. Such pros seem to outweigh the cons, or at least disguise them to some degree.

This constant demand for more is very self-centric. As the haves parade themselves on social media, the have-nots across the globe watch on their phones and decide they want this too, reinforcing the move to a global materialistic culture.

But let's return to trust. We all want to trust. As humans, it is in our nature. We trust the Sun will come up in the morning. We trust the moon will change phase over the month. We trust the cycles of nature and the physical processes of our planet. But where does our trust sit when it comes to the people we share the Earth with? Society forever increases its list of rules to abide by, to the satisfaction of lawyers and solicitors the world over. This, in turn, demands that we protect ourselves from litigation at every step of our affairs by completing waivers and consent forms, clicking "accept terms and conditions" or signing various legal documents that ultimately imply a lack of trust. A handshake, or *gentlemen's agreement*, used to be all that was required. I have no doubt that many still honour this but, due to the power of governments and the laws created, a handshake has no legal standing and must typically be backed up by a binding contract.

Although it happens in some areas, the days of leaving your house unlocked are generally gone. In fact, due to a fear of intrusion or robbery, there has been an increase in securing property with shuttering or barbed wire, installing cameras or alarms and keeping a dog as a deterrent and protection. As personal and home security increases, so does institutional surveillance, keeping tabs on us via street cameras, phone monitoring and tracking, recording internet searches and observing us with spy drones or satellites.

This lack of trust and the parallel increase in fear looks to be on the rise, as does the loss of faith in politicians, governing bodies and others supposedly with our best interests at heart. A day hardly goes past without a prominent figure or organisation being reported to have betrayed our trust by going back on a promise, saying one thing and doing another or abusing their power for self-promotion or self-gain.

And do we trust ourselves? Shouldn't we at least trust our senses? For millennia they have kept us from eating poisonous or unhealthy foods, have told us if something is hot and will burn us, warned us of approaching danger or alerted us to a far-off call for help. What about our other, perhaps less-developed senses, such as gut instinct, intuition or any perceived spiritual guidance? Have we developed these senses at all or learnt to trust them?

All the factors listed above are at play when we are growing up and continue to directly influence our lives, shaping us in one way or another into who we are now, becoming our blueprint for how to live. How we *think* we should live.

So how should we live? We have to accept, to begin with, that we are a product of our ancestors, our families, our schooling, our peers and our culture. Only in later life, when we are older and more independent, can we go out and discover more for ourselves and, if we so choose to, change our thinking, beliefs and any negative behaviours. As any smoker trying to quit would tell you, this is not easy. If the change is not out of a necessity, in the form of a life-threatening disease or imminent danger, then as humans, we seem quite content with the status quo. This is reflected in a general apathy for many world problems today. It is easy to defer to others, think of the problems as someone else's issue or believe that you, as only one person, cannot make a difference.

But we do want to make a difference. Looking for answers is built into our DNA. The time seems to have passed when we purely accept what we are told. There is too much that doesn't fit, doesn't feel right or is just plain wrong. Fake news isn't news, it is just a lie, a fabrication: spin to influence our thinking – ultimately to get us to like someone, buy something or give away our money. The bottom line is clear, the current way we are living and the current systems in place do not work. The world, and all life upon it, is in turmoil and a fight for survival, seemingly sadly moving towards catastrophe, not away from it. A change is both required and necessary, even if that change is just within ourselves.

Change can take place. Hence you are reading this book, have read others on self-improvement, life coaching, philosophy or religion, have gone on courses or retreats, watched hours of uplifting videos on the net, subscribed to various positive social media groups or websites that generate contemplative 'thoughts for the day', practice yoga or tai chi, meditate or have a wooden heart on your wall that says *'Love is the answer!'* Excuse the flippancy, but hopefully, you get my drift. We want to change. We want to grow.

Are there answers in being spiritual or seeking a spiritual life? Undoubtedly, but do you have to be spiritual or religious to live a good and productive life? The truth of the matter is that you don't. Not a dictionary definition of being spiritual or religious per se, as we all have a spiritual side, even if it is just a joy for life and a caring heart beating inside us that we listen to now and again.

Where are the tools and techniques to facilitate this change and explore what spirituality means in a non-religious context? Or what being connected to nature means without becoming a farmer, tree surgeon or vet? As we urbanise and spend more time in front of screens, our connection to nature and our relationship with the land has been eroded. But, as much as we have been turning our backs upon it, we are linked to all life on this planet. From the air and water that sustains us or the plant or animal-based food that gives us energy, to the relationships fostered with the animal kingdom or the multitude of landscapes and climates in which we live.

Living in harmony with the land, the environment we find ourselves in and the life we share it with (animal, vegetable and, I would say, mineral too) has always had its challenges. Ever since we first harnessed fire, we realised we could have some element of control over nature. Abusing this control has thrown us out of balance, given rise to power struggles, wars and famines, diseases and suffering. And with the increasing pace of industrialisation we are seeing forest decimation and wildlife species extinctions. We know a problem exists, but what do we do about it? Again apathy and the feeling of, *'What can one person do?'* may pervade. Well, one person can make an incredible difference, principally to themselves. That is where we all must start. Our relationship with ourselves.

Understanding more about who you are, who you want to be and looking at the areas you wish to change about yourself is no easy task. But it is possible: you *can* change and begin to look at things differently. By utilising tools and techniques similar to those used by your indigenous ancestors and working with the natural world, you can take great strides towards living the life you want to live. Changing your life is a process, and there will be difficulties, hardships, perhaps even times of loneliness, fatigue and pain, but the journey will be worthwhile and the rewards palpable.

The chance to live a life well lived shouldn't be taken lightly. You don't have to be anyone special, achieve anything in particular or reach a certain spiritual state, such as finding nirvana, heaven on earth or *touch the hand of God*. You just have to find that inner connection to life that has always been there. It was and is your birthright.

So how do you go about reclaiming your birthright and transforming your life? I am hoping that contained within these pages are ideas, exercises and practices that will help you. You do not have to follow them consecutively or complete them all. However, please read through the book and work with the ones that feel right for you. The ones that resonate. That said, I suggest the following should not be missed out:

- Create your own spiritual altar
- Life CV
- Release using an object from nature
- Transmuting trauma
- Conduct a memorial service for a loved one
- Ancestral lineage and cutting ties
- Inner child work.

If any of these sound daunting, don't worry, that's just your instinctual defence to the unfamiliar kicking in and maybe also emotion inside beginning to bubble up. It's time to let it go, free yourself and take the steps to *Change Your Life!*

Part 1
Introducing shamanism

*"We are all visitors to this time, this place. We are just
passing through. Our purpose here is to observe, to
learn, to grow, to love...and then we return home."*
Aboriginal proverb.

The Universe and *'what is'*

As much as we try to understand, categorise and describe the
Universe, there is always something more, always something
beyond our intellectual capability. But, of course, that never stops us
from trying to expand our knowledge. As Robert Browning put it:

*"Ah but a man's reach should exceed his grasp
or what's a heaven for?"*

Discoveries are constantly being made, along with updates to the list
of scientifically proven facts, both adding to and changing how we
comprehend our planet and the Universe. However, as we look to
return to the Moon, over fifty years since we first landed there,
scientists now classify 95% of the Universe as dark energy and dark
matter. That is, they do not know what else to call this missing stuff
that must be there to fit the equations. At the other end of the scale,
the study of the small is throwing up new theories, such as in the
field of quantum physics, changing how we understand interactions
at a minute level. The Universe, however, is whole at this moment.
It is behaving naturally. Science will say this behaviour is according
to scientific laws, and I believe that to be true. In the areas where we

currently do not have a scientific explanation, perhaps the science is lagging behind. Maybe we do not have sensitive enough measuring devices, are not analysing the appropriate data or are not looking in the correct area. A line from the poem Desiderata (printed in full towards the back of the book) sums it up beautifully:

"And whether or not it is clear to you,
no doubt the Universe is unfolding as it should."

Science can tell us one thing, but that picture is not complete. Nor will it ever be. Science and our understanding of the Universe will forever be expanding. We will never *know* it all. We can always look to a larger or smaller level by developing increasingly sensitive instruments or new detection methods. For example, discoveries at the minute quantum level are revealing new exotic particles, new building blocks for our model of how the Universe works. But these particles have always existed. Just because we had not seen them, could not detect their presence or understand their influence did not mean they were not there.

Conversely, new technology can also help us make discoveries on a larger scale, probing further into the distance, looking deeper into space and therefore back in time. Seeing the light from a star that is five billion light years away means we are looking at radiation emitted five billion years ago. In fact, with the detection of the cosmic microwave background radiation, we can look back to the dawn of the Universe and the Big Bang itself. Again, this radiation has always been there, even though it has only relatively recently been discovered and labelled by the scientific community. As the James Webb space telescope comes online, replacing the Hubble telescope as our most powerful eye on the night sky, we will be able to look back further than ever before and, undoubtedly, some incredible new discoveries will be made.

Gravity, similarly, has always been there. It may have been Isaac Newton (arguably on the back of Johannes Kepler and Robert Hooke's work) that gave us a mathematical formula to calculate gravity's strength, but this force was recognised long before the European enlightenment. Aristotle put forward the idea that objects moved to their 'natural place', as he called it, to explain why things fell to the ground. But it is likely civilisations before the Greeks knew there was a *pull-things-down-to-earth* force. They may even have had their own word for it.

Much has and will continue to be unearthed by science, but this will always be a subset of "*what is*". In the diagram below, *what is* represents all that is and ever will be. An all-encompassing definition of everything. Everything known and unknown. There is nothing more outside of this boundary. Within the boundary is human knowledge: all we as a species know and have ever known. Science and what science knows to be true, is a subset of this entirety of human wisdom.

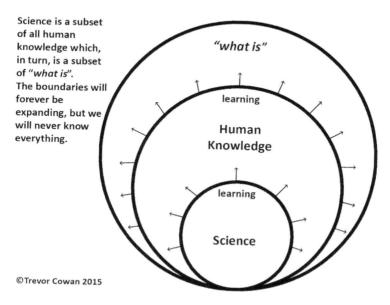

Science is a subset of all human knowledge which, in turn, is a subset of "*what is*". The boundaries will forever be expanding, but we will never know everything.

©Trevor Cowan 2015

31

There is knowledge and truth that lies outside the current limits of science, as yet unproven, maybe awaiting scientific discovery. It is within this area that some ancient wisdom and indigenous knowledge sit. It is where various shamanic and spiritual practices reside, often on the boundary with science, sometimes far from it. This does not make them untrue. However, they will not stand up to scientific rigour and are, therefore, quickly (and understandably, I might add) dismissed by the scientific and logical communities.

Nonetheless, useful knowledge, wisdom or truth does not need a scientific stamp to make it valid. There is knowledge that lies outside of the current (and ever-expanding) boundary of science – truths yet to be unearthed or proven – and there is no reason why we cannot tap into this well of wisdom.

We are here today because our ancestors survived. They lived long enough to pass on their genes and raise a family. Hundreds and thousands of generations culminating in us, the most evolved humans ever. (Although, as we look at the current state of the world, some may argue of a recent devolution.) We can work in the realms beyond science, add to our knowledge and experience, discover truths for ourselves and pass on our own teachings, just as people have done for millennia. Wisdom, ancient or otherwise, does not always fit inside the proven world of science.

We understand more each day, unearthing new pieces to fit into the scientific jigsaw describing how the Universe works. One day, we may have a complete scientific explanation of the Universe, *The Theory of Everything*, as physicists call it, but I doubt that day will be tomorrow or even one hundred years from now. So, basing our total understanding of life on science, as accurate as it is, may not be showing us the whole picture. What is still missing from the picture of life, the Universe and everything...?

Shamanism and land connected cultures

Throughout human history, there have been those that have lived in total connection to the planet, fostering a relationship with *Mother Earth* and the life upon her. Many indigenous peoples and tribal societies continue to follow their ancestors' ways by living in harmony with their environments, in tune with the natural rhythms and cycles, and knowing how to respect, nurture and honour the land. Within these communities, there will be one or two individuals who have been called to go a little deeper with this Earth connection and become spiritual leaders of the community.

These people often have gone through tremendous trials to understand their place within their culture's spiritual framework, as they learn to work with the energies of the land and the planet. Often they had traumatic or difficult upbringings, and may even have been seen by the community as being mentally unbalanced to some degree. In modern parlance, they did not fit in, had an alternative viewpoint on the world and were probably sensitive as a child – introverted, even exhibiting signs of autism or ADHD, but still creative, in their own way.

They have been given many names, from shaman to mystic, soothsayer to healer, medicine woman to witch doctor, witch to wizard, priestess to pastor. All have a connection to something bigger than just themselves. When this realisation is made, they understand it is their duty and life-long path to develop their connection to earthly nature (or the *more-than-human world*, as first coined by David Abram[2]), be of help to the community, honour and respect the land and provide spiritual guidance for all who need it.

---

[2] David Abraham, *The Spell of the Sensuous*, 1996, Pantheon Books.

Shamanism, in all its forms, was the ancient method by which people understood the world and linked themselves to it. It was arguably the precursor to religion. Ancient shamans realised there was an energy to all living things: a spirit, if you will. This is easy to grasp when it comes to the spirit of an eagle, soaring up high above the canyon wall, but harder perhaps when it comes to the static nature of a tree or, more so, that of a rock. However, as science has proven, at the level of the very small, all things have an energy; a vibration – even the rocks.

Over the years, shamanism has taken many forms but has always been based upon an underlying spiritual connection to the land. It is not magic or mystical but real and useful, often like common sense. The word shaman comes from the Siberian Evenk people as a general term for a tribal healer, with Core Shamanism being brought to the West by Michael Harner in the 1980s, and his book, *The Way of the Shaman*[3], becoming the bible for those that wished to embark on this path. It is from these roots contemporary shamanism became popular in the Western world, as many people, myself included, were looking for answers to some of life's more esoteric questions without the need to subscribe to mainstream religion.

Of course, trying to describe, categorise and explain a mystical and spiritual tradition that has survived for millennia will never be clear-cut. Everything is open to interpretation, and as each of us follows our chosen path, we naturally put our own take on the lessons, practices and teachings encountered. However, to my mind, shamanism is akin to an ancient form of psychology, based in and around nature, evolved (and continuing to evolve) from the natural world.

---

[3] Michael Harner, *The Way of the Shaman*, 1980, Harper & Row.

Evolution is a slow process and our development as human beings has taken time. For millennia we were content living off the land, and in our early nomadic cultures, when resources ran low or the weather conditions became unfavourable, we moved on. Eventually, we settled, domesticated animals and farmed the land. The animals local to the community were revered and honoured. They would provide food, clothing and tools (fish, boar or deer, for example) or be thought of as otherworldly, like the birds flying high above or the aquatic life forms that survived underwater. Making a spiritual connection to such seemingly miraculous creatures was not a surprise. Adorning oneself with clothing, head-dresses or ornaments made from these animals was symbolic of the respect the people had for them, and helped when worn in ceremony to embody the energies of these sacred beings.

We learnt to adapt to the seasons and stockpile resources for times of scarcity. Stories relating to many life experiences were passed down orally, generation to generation, from origin myths and survival techniques to connecting with the more-than-human world and fostering community. The stories may have changed over time, possibly becoming a little embellished, but the inherent lessons – the teachings – stayed intact. Not only were the lessons proven, but the teacher knew it was their duty to keep them alive for future generations. Giving thanks for the knowledge passed on by our parents and grandparents was the norm. Honouring them became routine, even ritualised.

Over time, these practices and teachings were brought together into a syllabus, a group of lessons that were the spiritual medicine necessary for the individual and community to stay in balance and harmony with themselves, the land and the energies that pervaded all life. A medicine wheel of wisdom. Such medicine wheels are still prevalent today, as the lessons they contain are timeless.

The medicine wheel

The medicine wheel is a framework for spiritual guidance and growth, often used by nature-based indigenous cultures (most commonly of the Americas), typically divided into the cardinal directions of north, south, east and west. Each *direction* has a specific set of practices and lessons, with many medicine wheels using animal archetypes to represent and, to some degree, embody the energies and theme of that direction. The teachings of the medicine wheel offer the student a roadmap and the skills necessary to navigate it, to understand themselves more fully, comprehend their interactions with life on this planet and act as a gateway to being taught the tools needed to become a contemporary shamanic practitioner.

There are a variety of medicine wheels (or similar frameworks for sharing knowledge) across the globe. Each group of indigenous people would embrace their particular version, based upon the local geography and their specific traditions passed down the generations. Some practices will be well known and easily replicated. Others will be difficult and require courage to undertake, with a few even being kept secret within the community due to their sacredness or power.

However, there is often commonality to be found in the themes of each medicine wheel: letting go, facing fears, seeing the bigger picture, connection to the land, honouring yourself, honouring ancestors, stewardship of the planet, taking responsibility for your actions and celebrating the gift of life. These common themes are pertinent to everyone and delving deeply into these areas can unearth great personal treasures.

A place for ceremony within modern life

In the modern Western world, we tend to live in our own space, alone or shared with a partner or family, in a house, bungalow, apartment or flat. The family unit is fluid and many young adults (if they can afford it) will leave home as soon as possible, with the ability and freedom to live almost anywhere on the planet. Most of us do not live in tribal villages or small settlements anymore, meaning there is a lot more detachment and isolation from others. This separation also means that community spaces, where people can come together and celebrate life, are being lost, leaving it to organised religions to provide such meeting places. What if you are not religious, by not being raised with a faith or not being drawn to a religion? Where do you go for deep or sacred ceremony and ritual? The simple answer is to conduct them yourself, at home or in nature. Sadly we tend not to be drawn to ceremonies we carry out ourselves, mainly because we have never been taught how to, outside of a religious context. However, we probably undertake a variety of rituals without even realising it.

Rituals are actions that are repeated regularly or are part of a daily spiritual practice. They can encapsulate an informal process, such as how we go about our morning ablutions or our method of making a cup of tea, or have a more symbolic meaning, such as lighting a candle before meditation, touching the earth before competing in a sporting event or patting the door frame before leaving home. Sitting around the dinner table is a good example of a simple ritual. The family sharing what has happened in their day, connecting to each other and maybe giving thanks for their meal by saying grace.

On the other hand, a ceremony is built around a specific purpose, i.e., a birth, marriage or funeral, and can be used for personal spiritual connection and growth in other areas such as letting go, honouring nature or connecting to the Divine. In fact, a ceremony can be held for pretty much anything. Recognising there are stages in life people go through, problems we all face and difficulties that come with being human is more important now than ever. Our issues, wounds and struggles are not the same as they were for our grandparent's or even our parent's generation. They have changed in line with the rapid shifts we have seen globally over the past few decades. Ceremonies can help with dealing with these changes.

If you have been lucky enough to come from a good family in a safe and resource-rich country, then your ability to see challenges clearly, and deal with them effectively, has been given a good start. If your upbringing was not ideal, then there may be weaknesses in your ability to cope. This is where the support structures of family, friends and society should kick in – to provide buffers for these shortfalls. Not just plasters to cover the problem but real healing to get to the core issue and resolve it, unearthing the wisdom of the lesson to be learnt.

This caring community side of life seems to have taken a back seat in the UK and the westernised world, in line with the increase in people and families living separately. There is also a general decrease in the human interactions necessary to live, as more time is spent online: conducting business or in meetings, watching entertainment, shopping or ordering food to be delivered to your door. Indigenous cultures, however, historically have community ingrained into their way of life. Be it sitting in a circle together in council, talking with elders, conducting rituals, rites of passage, honouring the ancestors, respecting each other, recognising the sacred feminine and masculine or connecting to the spirit of the land. There would also be time devoted to just celebrating life and being in that childlike state of wonderment and innocence that comes with truly seeing the beauty and majesty of the natural world.

This behaviour may seem like a long way from competitive urban town/city life where science, logic, money, efficiency and speed rule. But with some effort, and a re-establishment of the connection to nature, these gifts – these birthrights – can be reclaimed. Ceremony is a direct link to this connection.

Plenty of life events mark transitions for us: being born, starting school, puberty, becoming a teenager, passing exams or graduating, reaching adulthood, getting married, a new home or job, birth of your child, retirement, death and passing over. Conducting some form of ceremony can help recognise, honour and ease these transitions. However, some rites of passage can seem barbaric to the modern world, especially if they involve pain or deprivation. For example, the Mawé people of the Amazon rainforest in Brazil believe that any boy who wants to become a man must experience the worst pain the jungle has to offer, the sting of *Paraponera clavata*, the bullet ant. The boy must wear gloves woven with dozens of bullet ants for five minutes, enduring excruciating pain as the ants repeatedly sting him. Afterwards, both hands and arms may be temporarily paralysed due to the ant venom, with the boy likely to suffer severe pain, convulsions or hallucinations, usually lasting for several days. The boys in this tribe may undergo this initiation process about twenty different times over several months before they can be considered warriors. Such extreme ceremonies are unfamiliar to most people and, I suggest, are not necessary in the world in which most of us live.

A ceremony can be used to let go of that part of your life that is ending, be it a career, relationship, home, pet, habit, foodstuff, treasured possession or even a way of life. If you feel like you are giving away or losing something, then a small letting-go ceremony can help the process and make you feel more at ease with the loss.

Ceremonies provide a structure for conducting spiritual work, be it bringing something new into being, asking for help with a current project, personal or global healing, guidance on life purpose or honouring the changing seasons or moon cycles. A ceremony magnifies the potency of an intention and provides a narrative to help those present carry out what they have to do. It provides a framework to step away from the mundane and into the non-ordinary, stating to the Universe that something important is happening.

Ceremonies can be elaborate affairs, sometimes lasting hours, days or even weeks, with all manner of ceremonial trappings, from special robes and elaborate wording to holy objects and religious relics. In truth, none of these are necessary, although admittedly, the wearing of ritualistic garments or using sacred objects can feel powerful and put you in the right frame of mind for conducting the ceremony. Such ceremonies have developed and evolved over time and, mainly due to the male egos involved, have often become overly ornate, decorative and, at times, rigid in their structure.

All that is required is an opening intention, doing the spiritual work and ending in gratitude.

Part 2
Contemporary shamanism

"Shamanism is not a course, but a life journey"
Alberto Villoldo.

Framework used

Shamanism, contemporary or otherwise, can only be touched upon in a book. If you wish to go deeper with shamanic work, you will need a teacher to work with directly. Ideally, study with others, so experiences can be shared. Often there is as much to be learnt from the other people in a group, as from the teacher. Actively seeking out guidance and authentic training is an acknowledgement that you are serious in your endeavours. It is similar with the exercises described in this book. Actively engaging in them will result in a more profound experience, over and above any comprehension from just reading.

As mentioned, the medicine wheel is a framework for spiritual teachings, often used by nature-based indigenous peoples. There are numerous medicine wheels (or similar systems) across the globe, each varying due to the geography and different cultures they represent. However, even with these differences (sometimes dramatic, i.e., Inuit geography compared to Australian aboriginal), they often have similar core teachings and practices, as the human relationship with the natural world and dealing with life's challenges are common themes.

The exercises and activities in this book are, to some extent, based upon the medicine wheel of the Q'ero paqos (spiritual leaders) of the Peruvian highlands, as taught to me by my shamanic teacher Skie Hummingbird. The same South American animal archetypes of snake, jaguar, hummingbird and condor to represent the directions South, West, North and East are also adopted.

The essence of these teachings, and wisdom from various other shamanic traditions encountered on my travels, are interwoven with lessons from many years of working directly with nature and the energies therein. These teachings provide a practical and effective framework for individual self-discovery, growth and a reconnection to nature and the world around us. Please note, out of respect for my shamanic lineage, I am not sharing within these pages any sacred teachings or practices that should be taught directly. Such knowledge would only be passed on as part of a shamanic practitioner training course. There may, however, be some similarities within the exercises presented.

The core of this book is split into seven sections (*the Directions*), representing the different areas of self-exploration and teaching. The four cardinal directions, *South, West, North and East*, followed by sections entitled *Mother Earth, Father Sky* and *The Centre*.

- *The South* is concerned with looking at the past and letting go; it is represented by Serpent.
- *The West* is working with death and facing fears; it is represented by Jaguar.
- *The North* is about magic, seeing the joy in life and honouring the ancestors; it is represented by Hummingbird.

- *The East* involves seeing the bigger picture; it is represented by Eagle or Condor.

- *Mother Earth* is acknowledging our connection to all life on this planet. All that is below.

- *Father Sky* represents that which is *beyond* ourselves, our connection to the Universe, God/Goddess or Great Spirit. All that is above.

- *The Centre* represents ourselves; the responsibility we have standing in sovereignty at the centre of our own medicine wheel.

My teacher, Skie, put it like this:

> *"Serpent clears the ground, Jaguar takes you deeper into your own personal jungle, Hummingbird moves you higher and seeks out the beauty and flowers, Eagle rises above it all. They are different perspectives of the same thing, ourselves and our journey through life. One is not better than the other. There is no hierarchy. When completed, we can sit in the middle and maybe visit The West from an eagle perspective. The wheel will help reorganise your life, any patterns and behaviours, in line with what is best for you."*

In some instances, the exercises associated with each *direction* may seem more suited to the psychologist's couch, because shamanism, as I have previously suggested, is akin to an ancient form of psychology. I would say psychology today has its roots in shamanism, as both concern connection. Connection to the self, to others and to that which is beyond our consciousness: be it our subconsciousness, a collective consciousness, universal or planetary energy, spirit or the Divine. Working through any self-help book is, by definition, working psychologically.

Basic tool kit

You probably already have many of the *tools* suggested, but if not, they are readily available at little or no expense. There is no need to have special objects – ones with a high value, deemed sacred, blessed by a guru or from a far-off exotic land. Of course, we are often drawn to beautiful or interesting items and that is okay. Trust your intuition. Remember though, the phrase "a bad workman always blames his tools" is just as pertinent in the spiritual and shamanic world as in any other.

Items required:

- A journal. Noting your thoughts and experiences pertinent to your journey can act as way markers in the future when you look back at the path you have taken and see how far you have come.

- Sustainably sourced incense, sage or palo santo[4] wood, for burning and smudging.

- A smudge fan. Usually made from feathers, to waft the smoke from burning sage or palo santo. A single feather found in nature can be used.

- Hand drum and/or rattle. You will want a hand drum or rattle at some point, but initially they are not required as recordings are available online. A rattle is easier to hold and use, and cheaper and less intrusive regarding noise than a drum, but either is fine. Find ones that sound right for you. You could even make your own.

---

[4] Palo Santo (*Bursera Graveolens*) is a native tree of Central and South America. Its name translates as "holy tree" with the wood producing a highly fragrant smoke when burnt.

- Fifteen and thirty-minute drumming and/or rattling audio files. These should be instrumental only. Available online.

- A blindfold to enter darkness, ideally a Mindfold (a foam padded mask with eye cut-outs for comfortable wearing) or similar.

- A small stick, about 30cm (12 inches) long. It should be strong enough to withstand some flexing but light enough to hold in one hand and tap over your body when lying down. It should *feel* right when you hold it. Whittle it, remove sharp edges or overly rough bark and knots, smooth it with sandpaper or leave it totally natural. Make it yours. (See the section on trees and wood.)

- Candles or tea lights.

- A self-supporting mirror that you can look into when sitting down.

- A small compass, so that you know the cardinal directions wherever you are – often available on a smartphone.

- An audio/mp3 player (a smartphone is ideal) and headphones.

Where possible, ensure these items are ethically and sustainably sourced.

Space to work

The exercises and processes described in this book are called *work*, as that is what they are, work upon yourself. Therefore you need a space to carry out this work. Ideally, you will have a room or area that can be dedicated to this. A place of calm and tranquillity where you can sit or lie down and not be disturbed. It doesn't have to be a separate room, but this helps. It could be your bedroom, study or conservatory, even a shed or separate building outside. Make this space meditative by decorating it appropriately, maybe adorning the walls with artwork that calms and inspires you. Create a relaxed ambience by lighting a candle, burning quality incense, sage or palo santo wood, or playing calming background music. There are no rules, this is your space. Update how it looks as often as you like, especially when you are drawn to do so.

Spiritual altar

This is a place, normally a low-lying table or shelf, covered with a beautiful cloth if you wish, where you keep your spiritual and sacred objects. You probably have a place, or several places, where you already put photos or meaningful objects. Try collecting them together to form your spiritual altar, locating it in your meditative space, so you can sit with it undisturbed and easily gaze upon the objects or choose one to meditate with. It can contain any objects or pictures relevant to you and your personal take on spirituality: religious objects, natural objects, trinkets and keepsakes, crystals, stones, carvings, photos of loved ones, totems, mandalas, etc. Anything that feels important, beautiful or sacred to you. Review it and change it as you see fit. It should be dynamic and reflect your spiritual journey.

Opening sacred space

Whenever shamanic or spiritual work is being undertaken, especially in a new environment, you should take a moment to set the scene and *open* the space where you will be working. This is known as opening sacred space. It is a form of prayer and a way of asking for help from that which is outside of yourself, be it the more-than-human world, God/Goddess, spirit, the Universe or maybe just your subconscious. If you are going to ask for help, why not ask for help from all around you? From the four cardinal directions, north, east, south and west, from below and from above? This is my method (and the one I was first taught), accompanied by a short prayer as I face each direction; kneeling on the ground for the *below* and standing, raising my hands over my head, for the *above*. When first doing this, I felt awkward as I asked for help from whatever is above, most often called Great Spirit, God or the Universe. My rational background in science and engineering meant I had not encountered or believed in anything like this before, so I felt a little fraudulent, as I still had no evidence of a higher power. No tangible evidence anyway. But I was in training. I was drawn to this path and to the teachings, so I went with it. As I progressed and opened up, my viewpoint altered. Opening space became easier, felt more natural and also more powerful.

Perhaps the most significant change was the humbling effect it had. When I started to mean the words of the prayer, I found emotions could move easily within me, and great releases would take place just by opening space. Realising I needed spiritual guidance, feeling worthy of receiving such guidance, trusting that the help would come and recognising that, to some degree, I was part of a long lineage of people who have asked for and received such help, was at times a little overwhelming. But, truly humbling.

It makes sense to me that asking for help from all around is the best and most all-encompassing method. But there are many other ways to open space, such as casting a circle with your finger, imagining helping energy coming to you from all around or asking for spirit, God, the Universe or whatever feels suitable to come and be with you. Just asking for help before meditation or whispering a prayer while kneeling at the foot of your bed, is sufficient if you deem it so. As with many practices, it is the intention that counts.

If you are cynical about working with (or believing in) God, spirit or any other form of intelligence or energy outside of yourself, why not accept that you are at least working with your subconscious: that part of your higher functioning that is continually operating, even if *you*, the conscious you, are blissfully unaware of it. Think of it as being similar to the physical processes happening continuously within your body that your consciousness is oblivious to (unless there is a problem), such as your digestive, endocrine or cardiovascular systems. Accept that your subconscious (and perhaps a super-consciousness) is at work while your consciousness gets on with day-to-day living and the experience of being *you*.

Asking for help is okay; accepting it is another matter. Our egos can be powerful and manipulative. Be careful not to fall into the ego trap of equating what you put in to what you expect to receive out. For example, praying twelve hours a day will not necessarily bring more significant results than a short two-minute prayer in the morning. Adorning statues of deities with flowers, food, alcohol or beautiful trinkets doesn't mean you deserve to be rewarded with a spiritual gift. It is not an equation to be manipulated.

The ego can also filter and distort information and sensory input, becoming a barrier to any help that may be forthcoming, by dismissing it as fictitious, fanciful or irrelevant. To limit the ego's effect, try putting yourself into a childlike state when undertaking spiritual work. That is, put yourself into a state of not knowing. One of awe and wonder and, most importantly, in a place of play. Playing is one of the most powerful ways children (as do most young mammals) learn some of the skills they will need in adulthood. It is no different in the spiritual arena, as spiritually, we are all children. If we were advanced, the world would not be in its current state.

So opening sacred space is talking to the unknown (or even the unknowable). It is talking to that which is beyond our consciousness, beyond what we are typically aware of, saying that we are here and ready to do some meaningful work, humbly realising that we do not know it all and, like a child, would like some help.

Here is a simple opening space prayer from the book *Rolling Thunder,* by Doug Boyd[5].

> *"Turn to each direction, look up and down,*
> *and ask for help.*
> *to the east where the Sun rises*
> *to the north where the cold come from*
> *to the south where the light comes from*
> *to the west where the Sun sets*
> *to father Sun*
> *to mother earth."*

The prayer I generally use to 'call in' the directions is shown below. It was gifted to me by my teacher, who, in turn, received it from her teacher. This version is for use within a group setting but can work individually too. I have modified the wording slightly over the years and would rattle briefly or give a couple of drumbeats before saying the words to each direction.

---

[5] Doug Boyd, *Rolling Thunder*, 1974, Random House.

To the winds of the South,
Energies and spirits of the South,
Great Serpent come,
Come wrap your coils of golden light around us.
Teach us to shed our skin the way you shed yours, to let go
Teach us how to walk softly upon this earth.
Show us the beauty way.

To the winds of the West,
Energies and spirits of the West,
Mother, sister Jaguar come, come from your lair.
Protect this medicine space.
Show us the way of peace,
To live impeccably.
Show us the way beyond our fears,
Beyond death.

To the winds of the North,
Energies and spirits of the North,
Royal Hummingbird come,
Show us the magic and joy there is in life.
Share with us your courage and dogged determination,
To keep following our epic journey,
Even if, at times, it means going sideways or backwards.
And ancestors, grandmothers, grandfathers,
Come, warm your hands by our fires,
Whisper to us upon the wind.
We honour those that have gone before us,
And those to come after us, our children's children.

To the winds of the East,
Energies and spirits of the East,
Great Eagle, Condor, come from your mountain top,

Protect us under your wing.
Teach us to fly high, to soar, to see beyond.
Show us the mountains we only dare dream of,
Our heart's true calling,
And teach us to fly wing to wing with the Great Spirit.

Mother Earth, Pachamama, our home,
We gather for the healing of all your children.
The ancient stone people,
The healing plant people,
The four legged, the two legged, the creepy crawlies,
The winged, the finned and the furred ones,
The sliders and slitherers,
The burrowers and cave dwellers,
our brothers and sisters,
All our relations.

Grandmother Moon, Grandfather Sky,
Star nations, God, Goddess, the Divine,
Great Spirit, Great Mystery,
Consciousness, super-consciousness,
You who are known by a thousand names and you who are
the unnameable one,
Thank you for bringing us together and
Thank you for allowing us to sing this song of life.

The most important part of any prayer is the intention and feeling, so choose words that resonate with you.

Closing sacred space

If you open sacred space before any ceremonial or spiritual work, it makes sense to close the space once completed. This can be done with a simple thank you to each of the directions and a general heartfelt moment of gratitude for any teachings that have come to you during the session. Closing space also acts to signify that you have finished working in/with the non-ordinary world and are now returning to the ordinary world.

Opening sacred space while on the move

You do not have to be in a fixed position to open sacred space. It can be opened at one point and closed at another – for example, if you are out walking in nature. Think of opening space as creating a gateway through which you can pass and then, as you continue your walk, carry out your intended spiritual work, walk in meditation or just connect with the nature around you. When finished, close this gateway by closing space, even if you are ten miles from where you opened it. In a crowded public place, you may want to use minimal movements to open space, maybe just turning briefly to each direction, touching the ground and gazing towards the sky as you recite your prayer softly under your breath.

Grounding

Much of the spiritual work described in this book involves visualisation, and connecting with something outside of yourself (or outside of your consciousness) in one way or another. When the work has been completed, you can sometimes feel lightheaded or a little disconnected. Generally, spiritual work carried out in nature is by its very essence grounding, but if you have not been *working* outside, then taking time to reconnect to the earth, to ground yourself, is worthwhile. Grounding helps bring you back into your body and be able to continue with your day without a *floaty* or *not present* feeling.

Grounding is especially important for people who spend a lot of time in their mind (due to their employment or lifestyle) or are detached from the land for long periods. As more of us live in urban environments and in flats or apartments, our connection to the land and the natural world is being eroded. Conversely, those living in the country, working with the land or spending a lot of time in nature will probably find that grounding is unnecessary. It happens naturally due to their already strong connection to the earth.

The simplest method to ground is to stand up and imagine roots growing out of your feet and being sent down deep into the earth. It doesn't matter if you are wearing shoes or away from the ground (i.e., on the 23rd floor of a building); just imagine the roots going down from wherever you are into the earth. Visualise the roots going deep and spreading out in all directions, connecting you to the planet. This is often enough, but if you want to go further, visualise energy, maybe in the form of a colour, coming up the roots from the earth into your feet and body, energising and strengthening your earth connection. Breathe this in on the in-breath and let go of any negativity or disconnect on the out-breath. A few cycles of breathing should be enough to feel *back in your body* and grounded.

Having a warming drink or something to eat is also grounding and especially worthwhile if there are major shifts during your session.

Visualising and using your imagination

Many of the exercises described in this book call for some form of visualisation, a way of seeing things in your mind by imagining scenarios or events, perhaps merging them with actual memories. Being relaxed and in darkness (by using a blindfold) can help with visualising, as can using a repetitive drumbeat or rattle sound.

Our minds are powerful and can be used to stimulate physical changes. My dad has often mentioned how he can warm his cold feet just by thinking them warm. Try imagining a warm tropical sun bathing your body if you are physically cold or a cooling breeze wafting over you if you are overly hot.

Visualisations are also helpful in many areas of self-improvement where a goal is to be achieved, from sportsmen and women visualising themselves winning to politicians rehearsing public speaking engagements or entrepreneurs envisaging a successful business. The power of visualising and creating a successful outcome in your mind is not to be underestimated.

However, not everybody imagines or visualises in the same way. In fact, some people find it very difficult to *see* things in their mind. So try this exercise. Imagine an orange. Now imagine it cut in half and imagine the smell, perhaps even the taste. Get your juices flowing. Now imagine an elephant. Imagine it standing on an orange. Shrink the elephant. Make the orange big. Can you change the elephant from grey to orange and the orange from orange to grey? Try imagining the orange's flesh as purple, the outer skin silver and, instead of pips, visualise diamonds dotted within the segments. If you can imagine this, you can imagine anything with a little effort. On the other hand, if you found this exercise difficult, try working with your other senses. Maybe you can feel or sense a situation or scenario, can taste the orange, for example or hear the elephant. Also, look at how you recall dreams and use this method when asked to visualise in the exercises. Trust that whatever way you imagine is right for you.

Shamanic journeying

In the shamanic view, there is a non-ordinary reality beyond our everyday physical world that can be accessed using shamanic journeying. All indigenous cultures have their ways of journeying and their own non-ordinary landscapes to journey within, such as *The Dreamtime* in the Australian aboriginal tradition or *The Otherworld* in Celtic shamanism.

Shamans go into a trance-like state when they go on a journey to connect with their spiritual allies. They enter this altered trance state using a repetitive drumbeat, rattle or song, sometimes aided by medicine plants (see *Mother Earth* section). The journeying I am describing is slightly different, namely a form of active meditation. Meditation takes the meditator away from their thoughts, giving them a break from the usual mind chatter. Shamanic journeying is far more of a dialogue, used to obtain information and find answers to questions. It is a dialogue with, if nothing else, your psyche or subconscious, and often filled with metaphor and symbolism, generally more concrete than that of a dream.

To journey effectively, you need to occupy the part of the mind that wants input. In meditation, this can be achieved by using a mantra or the breath. Silently repeating the mantra to create an almost trance-like state or gently focusing on the breath, noting the coolness of the air entering the nostrils on the in-breath and its warmth on the out-breath. In shamanic journeying, a similar *distraction* is needed, but in this case, it is a constant beat or pulse, commonly provided by a drum or rattle. A blissful trance-like state can be achieved when allowing this beat to act as a focal point for the mind, becoming the heartbeat of the journey. In shamanism, the drum is often referred to as having horse energy or spirit, as it is upon this beat that the practitioner *rides* and is transported to *other* places.

Going into darkness is a key part of journeying, either with your eyes closed, wearing a blindfold or venturing into a dark place. Caves or specially constructed dark chambers, such as sweat lodges or kivas[6] were (and are) used by shamans and spiritual workers to journey to the non-ordinary world and conduct their rituals and ceremonies. Of course, accessibility to caves and dark spaces in the modern world is limited. However, with a little effort, you can make a room practically lightproof by using blackout curtains, combined with a window plug made from cardboard, foam or similar, and rolled-up towels for any gaps at the bottom of doorways.

Finally, setting an initial intention to provide a definite purpose is good practice. The intention can help guide the journey and is something to focus upon when, as is often the case, you may be distracted by a noise back in the ordinary world, or hijacked by a stray thought about dinner, for example, and brought out of the journey. As with meditation, let such thoughts and distractions pass, return focus to your intention and allow yourself to be taken away again on the beat of the drum. With this constant beat, you can visualise landscapes and scenarios, keeping in mind your intention, and journey to seek information and answers to your questions.

Shamanic practitioners will use journeying to connect with their spirit guides. These can take any form, be they human-like, ethereal beings or known or fantastical animals. Animal spirits are often

---

[6] a kiva is chamber, built wholly or partly underground, traditionally used for religious rites.

consulted because, as humans, we have a strong emotional, physical and evolutionary relationship with the animal kingdom. In the journey within this non-ordinary reality, there are no physical rules. We can explore any place, go to any time, be comfortable in any environment and be visited by any manner of being or animal, communicate with them and be taken on a journey with these spiritual allies as our guides.

Types of shamanic journey

There are generally three types of journeys in the shamanic practitioner's tool kit: the lower, middle and upper-world journeys.

A lower-world journey can be helpful with past events to access your subconscious and work on personal transformation at a soul level. It begins by visualising yourself going downwards, generally through an opening in the earth, such as an animal burrow, a cave, a rock crevice or tree hollow, maybe even down a waterfall, into a well or diving to the ocean depths. It is usually a place where helping animal spirits can be found. A literary example of a lower-world journey is Lewis Carol's *Alice in Wonderland*, where Alice has her adventures after going down a rabbit hole.

An upper-world journey is about connecting to your higher self and seeking guidance from spiritual teachers, be they ascended masters, gurus or the Divine. It is a place for personal enlightenment and to see future possibilities. The journey begins with taking yourself upwards, be it climbing a tree, rope, ladder or stairway, jumping skywards from the top of a mountain, soaring up in a hot air balloon or being taken away by a tornado, like Dorothy's journey to Oz. The journey continues upwards, breaking through layers or boundaries until the non-ordinary upper world is discovered, often a fantastical place amongst the heavens. There may be gates to be passed through, giving access to a celestial world, often with a castle or city in the sky; an Emerald city in the case of *The Wizard of Oz*. Another literary example is Jack climbing the beanstalk, discovering his upper world is home to a giant.

If the lower-world journey is earthly and nature-based, the upper-world journey is ethereal and otherworldly. More often than not, the spiritual allies encountered in the upper world may appear more human-like, but this is not a rule. Additionally, when you embark on a journey to one world, the journey may take you to another. This is okay. Trust you are visiting the right place and allow the journey to unfold as it wants.

The middle-world journey takes place in this realm, in locations you can physically visit. It is a journey to more deeply understand your role within this world and connect with the nature around you. The journey is to simply be in a place you know, such as your garden or local park, and commune with the animals, plants and trees. This type of journey can be done, for example, when sitting on a bench in the park or walking meditatively in the woods while connecting with the flora and fauna.

These three worlds are often symbolised by a 'World Tree', also known as the *axis mundi* (a mythological concept representing the connection between Heaven and Earth or higher and lower realms.) The tree has roots going down into the earth representing the lower world (gut feeling, connection to soul, for help with emotions deep within yourself), the trunk is the middle world (here and now, reflecting back to us at eye level, easy to touch) and the branches reach high towards the upper world (asking for help from guides or teachers, outside of ourselves, our higher self).

There are plenty of online resources or books on shamanic journeying if you want to understand more, and, as with all activities, your confidence will grow with practice.

Outline of a short shamanic journey

The below is a general outline of a shamanic journey you can try for yourself. There are also narrated journeys available online (or on my website *ShamanicHelp.org*) that can be followed.

You will need an intention for the journey. What is it that you want to work on? A couple of simple intentions are, *What do I need to know today? Or What is my spirit animal?* But they can be deeper, depending on your level of experience with journeying. Animals, our relationship to them and the energy or spirit they embody, are a cornerstone of shamanic philosophies. A spirit or totem animal is an animal we have a strong connection with (sometimes lifelong) and whose spirit wants to be with us, to teach or show us something relevant to our journey.

Be in a peaceful, safe space where you will not be disturbed. Firstly open the space as previously outlined or however you see fit. Lay down or sit comfortably and put on your headphones, ready to listen to a shamanic drumming instrumental audio file that is no longer than thirty minutes. Set the volume to your comfort level, but I suggest having it so that the drumming is in the background and not drowning out your thoughts. Use a blindfold or similar to go into darkness. Relax, take some calming breaths and begin listening to the drumbeats.

Start by visualising yourself lying down in a beautiful place in nature, maybe a real place, perhaps from your childhood or a totally fictitious place. It doesn't matter. Take a moment to feel the grass or ground under you – supporting you. Feel safe here. Notice the smells, the sights and the sounds of nature around you. Feel the warmth of the Sun on your face and body. Feel at peace, supported and relaxed. Spend time acclimatising and becoming familiar with this place in your mind.

When you are ready, visualise yourself standing up from this spot in nature and start walking. See a path ahead of you and walk upon it. Notice the sound of your footsteps. After walking for a little while, see a wooded area ahead of you. Follow the path into the trees. Be aware of any changes in sound, temperature and smell. Continue walking through the trees until you see the path open into a clearing. Enter the clearing and see a stone circle towards the middle; a circle of stones about ten metres or ten yards across, with a beautiful tree in the centre of it. Walk into the circle and stand next to the tree in the middle. From within this circle you can focus on your intention and deepen your journey.

The journey will depend on your intention and can be as simple as asking to meet your spirit animal or be more profound such as connecting with ancestors, cutting past ties or meeting the Divine. This stone circle is a safe and sacred space. A place to do your spiritual work. Be humble in this place as you are asking for help; help to gain insight, to shed something that no longer serves you or help to grow. Be respectful but do not lose the childlike wonder and awe of being in a magical place. Be open and allow whatever wants to come up, to come up. If there is emotion, don't fight it – go into it. Let it come out and release it. You may leave the circle on your journey, be transported somewhere else or be taken to another place. You may even find yourself transformed into an animal or a non-human being as part of the journey. All of this is OK as you can be anything, communicate with everything, go anywhere and to any time while in this liminal place.

For a lower-world journey, start by going down in some way from the stone circle, for an upper-world journey, initially go upwards. However, during each journey, you may be taken in another direction. This may seem confusing, but as long as your intention is clear, let the journey unfold as it wants.

For this journey, we shall use the intention to visit the lower world to meet your spirit (or totem) animal. So, while in the stone circle, look for a way to go down into the earth. For example, through an animal burrow at the base of the tree. Feel yourself go down into the hole in the earth, pushing past the tree's roots and through a narrow tunnel, forcing your way deeper underground. Feel enclosed, surrounded by the earth as you move further down. After a period, see a light at the end of the tunnel that, as you approach it, opens out into the entrance to your lower world. Allow yourself to pop out into this world, almost in a symbolic birthing. This lower world can take on any appearance but is commonly a beautiful natural landscape. You may even find yourself back in your stone circle, which is fine. Take a moment to orientate yourself and take in your new surroundings.

From this place, call out and ask for your spirit animal to come to you. See, feel or imagine an animal coming to you from the trees, the air or the ground. There may be many. Ask each one in turn if it is your spirit animal. If it says "no" or doesn't feel right, then thank it for coming and ask again for your spirit animal to come to you. When you feel you have the right one, ask it a few questions. Maybe find out its name and ask why it has come to you. What does it want to show you? Your spirit animal will likely want to take you on a journey, and you may even find yourself transforming into the same animal, thus deepening the connection. Go with them, knowing it is safe to go wherever and whenever they wish to take you. Give yourself permission to drift and flow with the journey, exploring the landscape as it unfolds in your mind, your psyche, your feelings or however you are experiencing it. The more fully you can immerse yourself in this, the better. If at any point you come out of the journey, i.e., your thoughts drift onto something else back in the ordinary world, gently bring your awareness back to the drumbeat and focus on your intention and the journey.

When you hear the *call back* of the drum (the drumbeat will stop, pulse a few times and then become rapid), it is time to start coming back, as the journey is coming to an end. Quickly return to the stone circle, giving thanks to any animals, people or spirits that came to you during the journey, and for any teachings or messages received. Step out of the stone circle, back across the clearing, along the path through the trees, returning to your place in nature and lying back down. Allow the shamanic drumming track to finish, and slowly bring yourself back to your senses in the ordinary world by wiggling your fingers and toes, removing any blindfold and gently opening your eyes. Be in gratitude again as you come back into your physical body. Journalling any thoughts, messages received or insight given is often helpful. Remember to close the space when finished.

In the time after, the following minutes, hours or even days, you may see signs pertinent to your journey in the ordinary world. These can take the form of an image, a sound or a situation that resonates deeply with the journey you have just been on. These signs are gifts from the Universe/God/Goddess/spirit, showing that your efforts have not gone to waste and that you have been listened to. One such example is seeing a newly revealed spirit animal appear in a magazine, on a billboard poster, TV or the internet when you weren't actively looking for it. You might even receive contact out of the blue from a person that was in your journey.

Maybe look at such coincidences as confirmation that you are part of something bigger.

The shamanic process

If you are undertaking any shamanic or deeply spiritual work, the below is a generalised outline of the process to follow.

- Be in a safe, comfortable space where you can work undisturbed with your tools to hand.
- Mute your phone.
- Create the right atmosphere. Light a candle, smudge the area and yourself or play some appropriate background music.
- Set an intention for the work you are about to undertake.
- Open sacred space.
- Feel the connection to those you have called in, be they ancestors, animal totems, spiritual beings, a higher consciousness, the Divine, etc.

- Do the work based on your intention. Remember to be playful and in childlike openness.

- Use your tools or a drumming audio file/cd to help with journeying and visualisation.

- Allow any releasing to happen. Do not block it. Tapping the belly, heart or throat areas with your fingers or stick can help the release.

- When finished, ensure some form of healing or soothing energy is pulled in to fill any gaps left by the releasing, i.e., visualise golden sunlight or silver moonlight filling your whole body. Place your hands where you feel they are needed to help direct this healing energy or light.

- Afterwards, spend some time in stillness while being in a place of gratitude.

- Close the space.

- Ensure you are grounded and feeling ready to continue with your day.

- Journal your experience for future reference.

- Keep an eye (and ear) open, for any signs from the Universe pertinent to the work you have just completed, over the following days. Use your intuition to discern a clear sign from noise.

The tools and techniques outlined in this section are aimed to help you with the work on yourself in the following chapters. Do not worry about making mistakes, missing something or doing an exercise differently. Holding the intention, being open and humble when doing the exercise and ending in gratitude are all that is needed.

Warning and disclaimer

Working on yourself is challenging and not for the faint of heart. You must be prepared to face yourself, "warts and all", as they say. Doing the exercises and practices on your own will require strength and determination, which is why they are described as *work*. They are work. Work upon yourself. You may feel that some of the exercises are better to do with another person or with the help and guidance of a trained shamanic practitioner. If you are drawn to working with another, please do so, as this can help you feel supported when going fully or more deeply into the process, but do try them at least once on your own first.

Be ready to reassess and even reject what you have previously learnt, some of which may be deeply ingrained. Trying to change a habit of a lifetime is tricky at best. This can lead to a grief process, grief for the loss of that previously been held onto as truth. Be prepared for this. Grief is OK. Sadness is OK. In fact, any human emotion is okay. What is essential is not to dwell on the negative emotions. Let them be springboards to a more illuminated, connected and authentic life.

Please be aware that I am not a trained medical professional. Any of the exercises or advice in this book should not replace professional healthcare or the guidance of your doctor.

There are also exercises presented that offer some degree of danger when undertaken, such as working with darkness, working with and under water, working with fire and looking towards the Sun with closed eyes. I am confident that common sense will prevail when trying any of the exercises, but I have to say that you carry out any of these practices at your own risk. Be sensible and err on the side of caution, but at the same time, have fun and play with the ideas, as we learn much through play. Potentially dangerous exercises are marked with **Note: Safety warning**. Please heed this.

Some of the exercises or practices can be done anywhere: on the bus, on the train or sitting on a park bench. Most, though, require some action, contemplation or visualisation, so your focus will often be elsewhere. Therefore, as the usual disclaimers say, do not try these exercises while driving or operating heavy machinery. Nor light machinery, for that matter!

Part 3
The Directions

The South - Healing the past

"Who looks outside, dreams. Who looks inside, awakes."
Carl Jung.

The direction of *The South* is represented by Serpent within the medicine wheel used as a general framework for this book. It is about letting go of what has gone before – shedding the past, just as a snake sheds its skin. Our past affects us in many ways, so the following exercises will help clarify your own history and illuminate where the focus of your inner work should be.

Life CV

In your journal or even in a computer spreadsheet, write down in the left column a consecutive list of the years you have been alive, starting from a year before you were born to the current year (2022 at the time of writing). For example, if you were born in 1971, write:

1970
1971 – born
1972
1973
...
2022

In this case, the list would be fifty-three lines long. Against the year before you were born, write down any major world event that was happening around the time of your conception or the situation your parents were going through during that period. Were they together, in love, married? Do you know? Can you ask them? If they have passed, is there another family member you can ask? If not, try to meditate or journey on this and ask to be shown more information. Against each of the other years, fill in key or major events in your life. Start with the most impactful events, such as traumas, births, deaths, relationships, illnesses, etc. Then add other significant life events, such as moving home, pets kept, schools attended or memorable vacations. Anything you feel affected you mentally, physically or emotionally is worth writing down. You may also want to include material objects, possessions or keepsakes, TV shows or movies, books, magazines or posters, etc., that you remember affecting or influencing you.

Keep the list handy, so you can add to it whenever something important pops into your head, as it is unlikely you will remember everything in one sitting. What emotions have been brought up by writing this list? Is there anything remembered that surprises you, anything that you feel is still an issue?

As creatures of habit, there are patterns in our daily lives. Are there any patterns in your *Life CV*? Does anything keep repeating? An example of a pattern when it comes to relationships is made evident by the expression, "I always seem to date this type of person", often spoken with a sigh of resignation.

Any major life event can influence us. It can shape us in one way or another, but not all traumas or upheavals in our lives are obvious. Yes, there is clear influence from the significant events listed on the *Life CV*, but others can be hidden and could have been playing out within our lives at a level we have been unaware of. Often these stem from events in our childhood and ones that perhaps we give little or no credence to. The death of a pet when we are young is par for the course in most children's lives, but what if it had an underlying effect on us, one that carries through into adulthood? Are we aware of this? Then there are the echoes of what we have inherited from our parents and their bloodline – genetically, and perhaps energetically. Fortunately, these less apparent influences on our character and life patterns can still be accessed and worked upon at a deeper level. However, some may require the assistance of a shamanic practitioner or similar to unlock them.

Additionally, as we all have at least one book inside us, your *Life CV* can act as a basis for your autobiography!

Letting Go

Trauma and wounds from the past can often be held onto. Over time, we begin to believe they are part of who we are, with the scars becoming badges. Badges that say what we have been through, what we have survived or how tough we are. These scars feel like part of us – prized possessions almost – and letting them go becomes difficult. Denial creeps in as to how much they affect us. It is not until we start digging into these wounds, that the true power of the trauma can be unearthed. Going to a psychiatrist or similar therapist is the usual route; spending hours *on the couch*, talking and chipping away at the issue, possibly re-framing it, and hopefully given the tools to understand and move on from the problem. But I believe the shamanic method is a faster, more profound and fuller experience that opens up a new pathway to understanding yourself, the world and your place within it – which, to my mind, is the whole point of any psychiatric endeavour anyway. The word psychiatry has its roots in ancient Greek: *psych* from *psykhē*, meaning 'soul', and -*iatry* from '*iātrikos*', meaning 'medical treatment' (from '*iāsthai*', meaning 'to heal'). Therefore, psychiatry literally means 'medical treatment of the soul' or 'heal the soul'. Doesn't 'heal the soul' sound like work involving the spiritual rather than just the mental or psychological?

Please note, I am not dismissing psychiatric help, and once again state that the exercises in this book should not replace any medical treatment being received or the advice of trained healthcare professionals, but rather be used as complementary and for self-discovery. To 'know thyself' (*gnōthi seauton*) is as important today as it was in Ancient Greek times.

Release using an object from nature

This exercise can be used when something comes up that you want to release – be it a person, a trauma, a job or even a bad habit – and can be used alongside any of the other letting go techniques outlined in this book.

Go out into nature with the intention to energetically release the person or issue you wish to work with. Open sacred space and walk around holding this intention in mind, *allowing* an object to come to you. It could be anything: from a stick, broken root, rock, fruit or nut, to a piece of trash or even a dropped item of clothing. If it is a particularly unpleasant person or event you are letting go of, the object may look ugly – possibly twisted, gnarled, dirty, rotten or jagged. Trust your intuition. You will know when the right object is found. However, do not take anything living, such as cutting off a branch or pulling up a flower. The object will be dead (from a biological point of view) and of little or no monetary value.

When you have your object, blow all the negative emotion and energy into it – all of the imagery and feelings around the person or issue. Take your time over this and deeply feel into it. If tears come, let them. Keep holding the object during any release. Rub it on the parts of your body where you feel the emotion sits or is stuck; the belly, heart and throat are the most common areas. Visualise the unwanted energy being pulled out of you. See the object as a magnet for all the negative emotions and feelings around the person or situation.

Once you feel this has been completed, decide if you want to work more deeply with the object (maybe trying the *transmuting trauma* or *clearing blocks using breathwork* exercises outlined in the coming pages), or if you wish to dispose of the object immediately, signifying that you are finished with the person or issue and any hold they or it may have had on you.

To dispose of the object, simply throw it away. Throw it away somewhere in nature, making sure it will not be found easily and do so with the intention of releasing the person or issue. Throw it with your full force, with a shout or angry expletive, and feel done with it. You're getting rid of something that no longer serves you; something you may have been carrying in your psyche consciously (or subconsciously) for a while. Do not throw it at someone, over the fence into a neighbour's garden or where people congregate. Throw it into the sea, a lake or river, a quarry, a wooded area, the undergrowth, a wasteland or even a public rubbish bin. Once thrown, turn away and leave the area, feeling lighter. Don't look back.

Ensure you feel grounded, any energetic gaps left by the release are filled with something positive (a warm feeling of self-love, for example) and close sacred space.

Cutting the ties

Cutting the ties can be used to energetically sever the connection between you and another person, whatever their relationship to you, however briefly you knew them, and whenever they were in your life.

We are connected to the people in our lives in various ways, genetically, emotionally and spiritually. The strength and effect of this connection depends on the relationship we have or had with the other person. For example, when a romantic relationship has ended, a tie to the other person often remains, especially if the split was not mutually agreed upon. This connection can trigger repeated emotions and feelings long after the relationship ends. *Cutting the ties* is a process to finalise the split and energetically allow us to move on. *Cutting the ties* can also be part of the letting go process around any negative people, toxic relationships and traumatic encounters or to cut the energetic link between you and someone in spirit, a past life, a harmful habit or a situation you wish to be free from. Below are two methods that can be tried, either together or separately.

For this first method of *cutting the ties*, you will need a stick about 30cm (12 inches) in length. Find a comfortable and private space and centre yourself. Open the space. Visualise the person or situation you are releasing in front of you to heighten the energy around the release.

Begin by pulling out imaginary threads from your belly button. Try to feel these energetic attachments to the person or situation you are working with coming out of you. Visualise them as unwanted energy, maybe even see them as black or a colour of decay. Visualise yourself gripping these threads in one hand, pulling them out and cutting them away with the stick in the other hand. See the stick as a sword, knife or light beam slicing down through the imaginary threads. Bring the handful of cut threads to your mouth and blow them away, out of the window or into nature, visualising the strands disintegrating and dispersing into the ether. Repeat this process until you feel you have pulled out all you can and no more attachment is left. Then place your hands over your belly button and visualise a soothing healing colour or light coming from your hands and filling your belly, replacing all that has been let go of with something beautiful and energetically nourishing. Do this until you feel balanced. Close the space, making sure you feel grounded.

The second method of *cutting the ties*, perhaps more suited to relationship attachments, is to use an imagined energy field around you, separating you from the other person. Once you have opened space, visualise a force field, bubble or aura around yourself. Then see the person you wish to release coming close to the edge of it, holding out a box. This box contains everything from your relationship with the other person – physical objects, emotions and feelings. See the other person offer this box to you, allowing it to cross your boundary so you may take it from them in your outstretched arms. By taking this box, you are energetically taking back all that is yours. Feel this. Whatever your feelings towards the person, calmly say to them, "thank you", and "goodbye". In your mind, watch the person turn and walk away out of your life. Deeply feel like you are letting them go.

Hold the box above your head, seeing it burst into flames and disintegrate into ashes or transmute into sparkling light to be carried away into the ether. Let go of all of the box's contents, especially if there is an object they have held onto, such as jewellery, a book, artwork, a car or even a house, that you feel is yours. The division and disbursement of larger items should have been agreed upon beforehand, possibly legally. So, now is the time to let all the objects go and move on. Allow the bubble to dissipate and return to the ordinary world feeling lighter. When finished close the space and ensure you feel grounded.

Transmuting trauma

As a complement to the *release using an object from nature* and *cutting the ties* exercises, the *transmuting trauma* process can be used to work with your life's main issues. From the list created in the *Life CV* exercise, identify the top three traumas, problems or situations you want to work to let go of. Acknowledging and confronting these traumas takes courage, and by letting go, I mean transmuting the emotions into energies that can be dissipated. The memory will remain, but its emotional charge should be eliminated or reduced considerably. Afterwards, albeit perhaps slowly, the memory will also begin to fade. These three traumas and the people involved are the ones you feel most profoundly affected you physically, emotionally and psychologically.

As with the *release using an object from nature* exercise, find a natural object that represents the first or biggest issue/person you want to work with and hold it when carrying out the stages below. This process has its roots in the Hawaiian process called *Ho'opono pono* (which translates as 'to make right'), but this is a far more simplified version.

Firstly, find a safe and private space to work in, preferably sitting at a table, ensuring you will not be interrupted. It may be helpful to have some background music or drumming playing.

Open sacred space. Take some relaxing breaths, close your eyes and imagine the person sitting opposite you. Wear a blindfold if that helps. If it is an issue with no others involved, then create a clear mental picture of the situation as you remember it and put that across the table from you. Alternatively, imagine yourself as you were during the incident and visualise that version of you sitting across the table.

Out loud, say to the person/situation:

> *I'm sorry.*
> *Please forgive me.*
> *Thank you.*
> *I love you.*

Do this slowly, concentrating upon and feeling each sentence.

- *I'm sorry.* Feel repentance even if you know you were not at fault. Take responsibility for what happened. Somewhere guilt sits between you and the other person. Maybe you are clearing for both of you. If it is a situation, let any remorse take over you. Let any tears flow or sobbing come forth. Even curl up on the floor if that's where the pain sends you. This is your time to release. Do whatever it takes to let it out from your body. Tapping the throat, heart or belly will help any release.

- *Please forgive me.* This shows humility. Again, even if you are convinced it was not your fault, take the higher ground. And again, most definitely feel this. Forgiveness clears the past. You are also asking for forgiveness for yourself at the time. Perhaps for putting yourself in that particular situation. Spiritually we are children. We are allowed and meant to make mistakes; they help us grow.

- *Thank you.* Be in deep gratitude. For the person, for the situation that has helped you grow, for the lessons learnt, for being you, and for being able to take this step.

- *I love you.* Say this to the person or the issue, and send as much love as possible out into the Universe. Realise that by saying this, you are saying that you love yourself too. Accept this love back for yourself.

It may also be helpful if you can 'see' (in your mind) the other person and notice how they react when you say each of the above sentences.

You may want to repeat this process to go deeper, realising this is not absolving anyone or anything from blame, but rather an approach to help let go of the trauma emotionally. Even if you know you are innocent of any wrongdoing – if you were 100% the victim – you can take this higher perspective and forgive from a place of love. Such an approach takes bravery and courage, reinforcing your commitment to, and love for, yourself. In her book, *The Power Within You Now!*[7], Sue Stone says:

> *"The process is to forgive yourself, thank yourself and send yourself love. By doing this, you erase the impact of the memory. As the suffering vanishes from within you, it also disappears from the other person or the situation."*

When finished, carry out the *release using an object from nature* process with the natural object you have been holding. Blow any residual emotions into the object and rub it over your body. Visualise any remaining negative energies being *drawn out* and absorbed by the object, before throwing it away somewhere it will not be easily found.

---

[7] Sue Stone, *The Power Within You Now!*, 2019, self-published.

Do this for each of the people/issues you want to release energetically. When you feel you have finished, spend some time in gratitude for what you have just accomplished. If you feel tired or emotionally drained, visualise healing energy being drawn in to fill any gaps left by the releasing, placing your hands where you feel they are needed to help direct this healing energy or light. Close space and ensure you feel grounded before continuing with your day.

The trauma of being born

From the moment of conception, life begins. The latest science points towards the ability of an embryo to feel, and have an emotional response while in utero, and therefore be open to trauma. Vivian Broughton, gestalt[8] psychotherapist, in her book *Trauma and Identity*[9], says:

"The cardiovascular system is the first organ system to develop and the reptilian brain is first to form on top of the spine. After about twelve weeks, the limbic (mammalian) brain forms on top of the old reptilian brain and becomes a means to an emotional life and the possibility of remembering that life experience. At some point, the embryo has an autonomy, a life of its own as it develops, responding to external stimuli but also to chemical and perhaps energetic stimuli."

"... Neuroplasticity, the way neurons and pathways are formed and reformed throughout life, can show how it is easy to split off a traumatic experience, to create a bypass, and see the physical result of a traumatic experience in certain neural connections."

---

[8] Gestalt is a holistic process. It regards the individual as a totality of mind, body, emotions and spirit who experiences reality in a way unique to themselves.
[9] Vivian Broughton, *Trauma and Identity*, 2021, Green Balloon Publishing.

Vivian also argues that we are all born to some degree prematurely, as our large brain and the relatively small size of the female pelvis is prohibitive to a pregnancy longer than nine months. It is suggested by Charles Bluestone[10], an American doctor and Professor Emeritus of Otolaryngology (or ENT) at The University of Pittsburgh, that gestation time should be closer to twenty-one months. (Try telling that to any mother or mother-to-be, and be prepared for a look that could kill!)

So how was your birth? Were you the first child, or had your mother given birth before? Had she had a previous miscarriage or abortion? Was your mother overly fearful during pregnancy and labour? What was the length of labour, were there any difficulties, were forceps used or were you born via caesarian? How was your mother afterwards? Did she suffer from post-natal depression? Did she feel loved and supported during the pregnancy and birth? Were you given the love you needed as an infant? Were you wanted?

Any negative experiences felt by you as an embryo, during labour or as a young infant (including those imparted to you via your mother), could have had a hidden resonance imprinted on your subconscious. This is echoed by Vivian, who says, "trauma causes a psyche split, burying the painful experience in the unconscious."

A ceremony to release any negative emotions from the time in your mother's womb, your birth and early life may be worth the effort, even if there is nothing painful in your conscious memory.

Transmuting deeper trauma

What about events where forgiveness is seemingly impossible? For example, prolonged mental or physical torture, war crimes, murder, child abuse or rape. Is it helpful to revisit and relive the issue? How

[10] Humans are born too soon: impact on pediatric otolaryngology, International Journal of Pediatric Otorhinolaryngology, Vol 69, Issue 1, January 2005.

do you forgive a murderer, a torturer or the man who raped you as a child? It will not be easy. If such a process feels impossible, try re-framing it. You are working on this because you want to be free of the emotion and the negative side of the experience that has, and probably still is, affecting you in one way or another. In this case, perhaps a more ritualistic approach would work better than the previously outlined pragmatic one.

If the incident happened when you were young, put your younger self across the table from you and try saying, "I'm sorry, please forgive me, thank you, I love you", as if you are apologising to your younger self for what happened. Maybe you feel you were not protected as you should have been by those meant to love and look after you. If you cannot face picturing your attacker or abuser as you remember them, try visualising them as a child, and see the pain they probably suffered when young that manifested in later life into the pain they inflicted upon you.

However, anger, hatred, thoughts of vengeance or similar emotions are sure to surface. Are you strong enough to go beyond these, to send love to someone who has hurt you, done obscenely or abhorrently wrong to you? To perhaps break the cycle of pain that you are the victim of?

Such action is moving towards a biblical sense of forgiving sin and absolving all inflicted pain, taking tremendous courage and bravery to face and work with. If you have been through such a trauma and can work through the process, whether you feel healed or not, you have been truly courageous and can be very proud of making such an effort. Even a seemingly minor move in the right direction is progress, and often we do not realise the enormity of our perceived small steps and their echoes on our souls.

Again, it must be stated that there is help and counselling available from trained professionals who have experience with such devastating traumas. If you have not already, please seek such beneficial help with your issue. The work shared here should be considered complementary to any professional counselling (or similar) and hopefully offers additional ways of working on yourself to transmute emotional trauma so that you can move forward.

Clearing blocks using breathwork
Note: Safety warning

This process is based upon a breathing exercise described by Wim Hof, the Dutch extreme athlete, teacher and health guru. Ensure you are medically able to carry this out, as there is some strain on the heart and lungs. Do this exercise on an empty stomach and lying down in a quiet space, ideally after some yoga or light exercise to bring you into your body. You may find it beneficial to wear a blindfold or similar. As always, open sacred space.

Begin by taking a couple of breaths to relax into the process. Then take a full breath in, raising your belly first, followed by the chest. After inhaling fully, let the breath go naturally, not forcing it out or trying to empty the lungs completely. Then begin another deep full breath, expanding the belly and lungs to take in as much air as possible. Again, release naturally. Continue by repeating this cycle; full inhale, natural exhale. You may feel tingles in your hands or lips and possibly feel a little light-headed as you proceed. This is OK, but if it becomes overpowering, stop. When you have reached about twenty cycles, stop and hold your breath for as long as possible without straining. When you feel the need to take a breath, do so, then have a couple more calming normal breaths. This is one round.

Begin a second round of breathing and notice any emotion coming up or any blockage in the body that wants clearing. If there is, focus on this area as you breathe, perhaps tapping it with your fingertips. Tapping the place where you feel the block (usually the throat, heart or belly) can lead to a release, maybe as tears, shaking or even convulsive guttural sobbing. Often imagery will pop into your head, possibly relating to a past trauma, fear, person or difficult situation. Something that is associated with the blockage that also needs releasing and clearing. Decide then if you wish to go through another round, but typically, one or two rounds are sufficient.

You have taken yourself to the edge with the breath and, consequently, beyond the ego mind, thus lowering the ego's defences and allowing the release. You went to a vulnerable place where the mind is in less control. Fill the void left by what has been released with something beautiful: a healing colour, feeling, sound or image, or the energy of a loved one, a guru, master or deity. Whatever feels right for you. Nature abhors a vacuum, so replacing what was let go of with something positive is always best. However, being in gratitude afterwards, is often enough. When finished, breathe normally and allow yourself to come back into your body and feel grounded before closing space.

Taking oneself to the extreme, physically or mentally, has been, and still is, used by many as part of their faith or spiritual practice, be it breathwork, fasting, immersion in darkness, spending extended periods in silence, chanting, dancing, fire walking or arduous pilgrimage. All require focus, push the body to the limit and can be emotionally draining, but they loosen ego control, allowing space for connection to something bigger.

From here onward, I will not mention the opening and closing of sacred space or ensuring you feel grounded after an exercise, as this should now be fully ingrained.

Three perspectives

Three perspectives is a simple but surprisingly effective exercise to work with releasing the emotions and energy around a negative experience in your life, one that maybe you have kept hidden or are embarrassed about. When doing this alone, you will need a mirror you can sit and face.

Begin by reliving the experience, speaking to yourself in the mirror and giving air to the emotions around it. Speak about how it made you feel at the time and how you feel now. Talk to anyone involved as if they were there in the mirror. Go as deeply into the feelings as possible, allowing any emotions to be released. When finished, give yourself a moment to journal anything pertinent.

The second round is to retell your story, but this time from the perspective of what you have learnt. Share with yourself in the mirror the lessons taken from the situation or person. What insight has come from it? How has it made you stronger? If a person is involved, tell them what they have taught you while looking into the mirror. Again journal anything pertinent.

Finally, talk through your story with comedy, seeing the lighter side of the whole situation. Turn any tragedy, heartache or pain into something uplifting and light. Make it into something humorous.

By the end of this cycle of three ways of sharing the same story, you should feel lighter and less burdened by any emotions. This is a good example of re-framing – looking at an issue from different perspectives. Spend a moment in gratitude and journal as you see fit.

Alternatively, you could do this with friends or family members you trust. If they feel comfortable with the process, they can share too, but ensure everyone understands this is not about getting help or seeking advice. It is about being silent witnesses to each other. This may be difficult for others to do; not only being a silent witness but having to hear what you and others present say, as there might be guilt or shame if they feel they are somehow involved or connected to the issue. It may, however, just bring up sympathetic feelings within them, as it is human nature to empathise. Sharing in a group can also be very powerful, so take the opportunity to do so if it presents itself.

Letter writing

Letter writing is helpful with shedding light upon emotions around a situation or a particular person and to begin shifting these feelings. It can be especially useful if you are someone that spends a lot of time in your mind. Some typical examples are letters to parents, guardians, grandparents, your younger self, an ex-partner, an abuser, a loved one in spirit, God, Goddess or the Universe. But, in truth, you can write a letter to anyone or anything.

When writing the letter around an issue or situation, explain how you felt when it happened and how it affected your life. Also, describe how you feel now and how you wish to feel in the future, including what you want to let go of emotionally, physically or spiritually. If you are writing to a person, write to them directly, whether they are alive or have passed. Again, write about how they made you feel at the time, any effect their actions or words have had on your life and how you wish to feel in the future. Write from the heart. This letter should not be kept, as you would be holding onto the emotions rather than working on letting them go. The letter should be dispatched, either by posting or burning it. If you are going to post the letter, leave the front of the envelope blank so it will never be delivered. Also, do not write an address or any surnames of the people involved in the letter, ensuring it cannot be traced to them or you. Give a small prayer and offer thanks when posting the letter, sending it on its way with love and feeling any negative emotions attached being taken away.

If that sounds too daunting, perhaps the following option to burn the letter is preferable. Before burning, read the letter aloud, feeling the emotion it was written with once again, adding any more words and prayers you deem fitting before offering it to the fire. If a real fire is not possible, lighting the letter with a candle and dropping it into a fireproof dish is okay. Try to do this outside or near an open window so the smoke can be taken away by the wind, along with your prayers for the transformation and forgiveness the letter represents.

Releasing with water

Water is nature's cleaner. It washes away. Rainfall cleanses the land. Rivers remove debris and detritus. Drinking water flushes our system. We bathe with water. Using it spiritually is cleansing and healing.

Note: Safety warning
Working with water can be dangerous, especially if you go out of your depth, are not a strong swimmer or are working in fast-flowing currents, cold water, powerful waves or strong tides. Please be safe when attempting any of the below exercises.

Negativity wash off

Water can help wash away unwanted or negative energies or help let go of people, places or events from the past. Use the action of the waves, the current of a river or stream or maybe the pounding of a waterfall to wash away this negativity. Ideally, you should do this exercise physically: on the beach, in the sea, in a river, at a lake or under a waterfall. Of course, your location and the weather may make this impractical. If being in such a location is not possible, use your bath or shower, a hot tub or swimming pool or visualise the scenario in your mind during meditation. There are various options to work with the flow of water, as outlined below.

If on a beach, stand ankle-deep in the waves facing out to sea. Allow all you need to let go of to fall from your head and body, down and out through your feet, taken away by the waves. Visualise the outgoing waves carrying this negativity into the vast ocean before you. When comfortable with this, proceed to visualise positive energy flowing into you with the incoming waves, energising you from your feet and up throughout your whole body. Play with this cycle of ebb and flow. As you sink into the sand, feel your connection to the earth grow. Stay balanced and ensure you don't get stuck!

Similarly, if you are lucky enough to be on a warm beach, try lying down in the tidal zone, so the lapping water can reach your whole body without completely covering your face and affecting your breathing. Close your eyes and allow the waves' gentle action to wash away unwanted energies. Visualise whatever needs to be let go of flowing out from you as a colour, a feeling or an emotion. Allow this energy to be released by the gentle caress of the waves and washed away into the ocean. Again, with the incoming water, fill yourself with a positive feeling or energy. Through these cycles of ebb and flow, feel connected to both the earth below you and the water flowing over your body. Embrace this process as a physical and emotional cleanse.

A similar exercise can be carried out in still water, such as a lake, pond or swimming pool, ideally using a swimming noodle or similar flotation device. Find a comfortable position floating on your back. Then close your eyes and tilt your head back to submerge it, leaving only your nostrils above the water. With your face just under the surface, breathe calmly through your nose. Take time to get comfortable with this unusual position – under the water but still able to breathe. Feel the weight of the water on your face. Relax into this and let whatever you are releasing dissolve into the water as you calmly breathe. When you surface, do so slowly, feeling the water drain from your eye sockets and face, washing away further unwanted energy and leaving you relaxed. Repeat and play with this.

This exercise can also be tried in the bath, but will require some physical manoeuvring, probably with your knees up to give room to immerse your torso. If you do not have good upper body strength, this position could be difficult to get back out of. Please be cautious if attempting this.

When working with flowing water, such as a stream or river, ensure it is not too deep before stepping into the flow. You may need to wear boots or waders if the water is cold. Find your balance and stand still, allowing water to flow around your feet. Become comfortable in this position, adjusting your balance as necessary. Visualise the current drawing out and taking away whatever you are releasing, seeing negativity draining from your body and out of your feet into the flow of water. Visualise it dissolving and being carried away downstream. After, feel the water flowing into you from upstream bring in positive energy, replacing what is being let go.

A similar process can be used if visiting a waterfall where the water is warm enough to swim in. Firstly, manoeuvring yourself towards the waterfall will take some effort, and depending on the volume of water flowing, you may be unable to get underneath it. However, you should be able to get close and float nearby, listening to the thunderous roar and visualise your energetic body being purged and cleansed. Again, a similar exercise can be played with in the shower at home, using the cascade of water to wash away what is being let go of. If there is room, try sitting under the shower and working with the water flow here. As this is not the usual position adopted in the shower, the mind can focus more on the intention, improving the effectiveness of the process.

Alternatively, you can use visualisation to imagine yourself in nature, in the stream, the river, the sea, a lake, on a beach, under a waterfall, etc., and perhaps visualise the water not just as water but as a ribbon of light or a beautiful cleansing energy. Allow the flow to wash over you, removing what needs to be released and replacing it with something positive, nourishing and uplifting.

Sensory play like this activates and stimulates nerves, thus mimicking a feeling of release, of negativity being washed away. The scientific mind will say that this is all that is happening – a nerve activation, a physical sensation. But, when married with visualisation, this sensory play can create a powerful emotional response worth exploring.

Gratitude stones

Gratitude is a cornerstone of any spiritual and shamanic work. Once the work has been carried out, the exercise completed or the ceremony over, we should always give thanks.

Take a walk in nature, in your garden, if you have one, and find two small smooth stones. These can be used as your gratitude stones. Hold one in each hand, bringing the stone in the right hand over your heart. Close your eyes and give thanks for your life and anything you are feeling grateful for that day. Whatever comes to mind for you is okay, even if it is simply the blessing of another day. Repeat this every day. The stones will *grow* with this gratitude energy. Keep them on your spiritual altar or by your bedside as a reminder.

Some areas for gratitude are:

- Your home and neighbourhood.
- Your family and friends.
- Your job and career.
- Your health. We often take it for granted, especially when we are young. In later life, as problems may occur, health can become a priority.
- Fresh air and water. Again, taken for granted by most people in the Western world. But as industry and pollutants have infiltrated our lives, clean air and water are not always guaranteed, especially in impoverished areas.
- Your food. Give thanks before eating, perhaps with a blessing or prayer, showing gratitude for the journey your food has taken to your plate and the sacrifice made by the natural world so that you can eat.
- You. What are you thankful for about yourself? Focus on what you like and love about yourself. Self-love and treating yourself with gentleness can foster internal harmony.

Letting go of possessions

We all have objects, photos or keepsakes that we feel we must never part with, ones with a potent emotional charge associated with them. They usually remind us of a departed loved one or family member, a specific period in our lives or a particularly memorable moment – one we do not want to forget. There is something special about holding an object you know someone else has held or has given you with love. It represents a connection to someone or something in your past and carries with it an emotional energy. It is no different in the spiritual and shamanic world, as objects from nature can be used to hold and transmute energies, just as in the *release using an object from nature* exercise.

So why not for all objects? Indeed religious relics are deemed priceless by devotees of that religion, such as the Shroud of Turin in the Cathedral of Saint John the Baptist, Italy, the Beard of Muhammad in the Topkapi Palace Museum, Turkey, Buddha's tooth in the Temple of the Tooth, Sri Lanka or the numerous encased saintly remains (commonly bone or hair) locked away in churches and cathedrals around the globe. These relics are venerated by the faithful and have taken on an almost supernatural mystical power.

Heirlooms, of course, have sentimental and often financial value. To give away such items would seemingly be difficult for a couple of reasons. It may feel disrespectful to the family or the memory of the person who gave it to you or, from a financial perspective, it could be deemed wasteful, squandering what was bequeathed to you. However, this highlights the attachment we place on possessions. And not just heirlooms but many everyday items such as favourite clothes, a well-worn pair of comfy shoes, a cherished car or a house full of memories. Anything can be an origin of attachment. This is the Western way and undoubtedly true in the UK. Letting go of this attachment and letting the item go from our lives may ultimately be freeing but often challenging to do in practice.

So, firstly begin by having a clear-out. Part with all that can easily be let go of and is of little monetary value. Then progress to those items that fall into a *keeping just-in-case* category. Is it likely you will need it? Could you get something similar if required in the future? Then look at unused or rarely used items. Could they be given to charity? Look upon your gift as a way of passing on any joy the item gave you to somebody else. Apportion a financial value if you wish, and think of your donation as a monetary figure you are giving to charity. Finally, move on to items of value that are purely for decoration or are keepsakes. Which ones can you give away? Maybe give them to a family member, a friend or charity.

What items can you absolutely not give away? List them down and note the emotions that come up when thinking about giving each away. What is stopping you from letting these things go? Is it the memory of a loved one? A crossroad moment in your life? Do you feel you do not have the right to give it away? Is there a seemingly unbreakable promise around an item? There could be many reasons. Going deeper into these reasons can add more information to your *Life CV* from earlier in this *South* section.

Perhaps keep all your heirlooms together in an ancestor box. (See *The North* section.) If you feel brave enough, give away or pass on these items of sentimental and financial value. Note how you feel afterwards – lighter, regretful or a combination of emotions? Whatever the objects are, trust that they will go to someone who will enjoy or use them. You are, in effect, *paying it forward.*

Handover ceremony

If you have an item you cannot let go of, conducting a handover ceremony may be helpful. Firstly, be clear on why you are struggling to let the item go. Then find an object in nature, something natural you are drawn to, that can represent this precious item. A length of colourful ribbon, cloth or similar will also be needed.

The intention is to instil the energy of one into the other. Do this by putting the objects side by side on your altar and wrapping the ribbon or cloth around them, connecting both physically. Say your intention to swap the energies out loud and air any other thoughts or emotions around this handover, such as why you are struggling to let go of the treasured object. Leave both on your altar for a few days or until you feel comfortable that an energetic exchange has happened. Now you have two objects that represent the same thing. Is it now easier to give away your *precious* object? At a later date, it should also be easier to let go of the object from nature, whatever it represents.

For example, if your mother has sadly passed away and her broach is the only piece of her jewellery you have, the thought of giving it away seems inconceivable. So, while holding the memory of your mother in mind, you look for an object in nature and, for some reason, are drawn to an acorn. Placing the broach and acorn on your altar, cupped together on a beautiful purple satin cloth, you look at and hold both daily, remembering your mother fondly. While holding them, you speak out loud to your mother in spirit, speaking your truth, releasing any emotions and, at times, almost chatting with her.

After a week, you feel it is time to let your mother's broach pass to someone else, so you take it to your favourite charity shop, saying goodbye to it one last time. However, each day afterwards, you still look at and pick up the acorn, realising that the connection and love is still there, represented by this acorn. As time passes, the acorn on your altar gets lost, but you don't mind, as every autumn there is an abundance of acorns to act as a reminder of your beloved mother. In fact, whenever you see an acorn outdoors, in a magazine or on the TV, you are reminded of your mother, and a smile comes to your face.

Apologies to any mums who don't like the thought of being compared to or replaced by an acorn, so maybe a sea shell, poplar tree or even a garden bird, say a robin, is a better object of remembrance. Something that reminds you of your mother whenever you see or hear it.

Illness and disease

Illness, disease or any medical condition, whether inherited, caught or manifested over time, can take control of us and affect the quality of our life, even casting a shadow over how much longer we may have left on this planet. Unsurprisingly, such issues commonly become a focus for the spiritual, especially when mainstream healthcare is perhaps not as effective as we had hoped or wished for. Praying, meditation, visiting a spiritual leader or pilgrimage to a sacred place are accepted ways of asking the Divine or the Universe for personal help and healing. But there is more you can do for yourself that, if undertaken with openness and sincerity, can have profound effects.

Some believe that at the root of any illness is a spiritual issue, something we need to look at in this life, learn any inherent lesson from and heal in one way or another. It may show us, for example, where we are out of balance with our true nature or are holding onto the emotion of a past negative experience. An ailment can be eased or even cured when focus is given to the appropriate area. From the exercises in this book, obvious issues such as traumas and losses, along with other more subtle events or imbalances, can be highlighted and worked upon. This work at a spiritual level has a knock-on effect on the physical body. Sometimes the benefits can be felt instantly or overnight, especially emotionally or mentally. Often though, it takes time for the physical to catch up, but that doesn't mean instant physical healing is impossible. Miracles can, and do, happen.

Firstly, you must want to be helped or healed. Over time we may overly identify with our disease, illness or condition, especially if we have lived with it for several years. The ailment or issue becomes ingrained into who we are, becoming our *cross to bear*, even defining us to some degree. My journey with tinnitus has provided many moments of introspection, ranging from the illuminating to the fearful, and most commonly returning to the spiritual explanation of "not listening", as my tinnitus is a high-pitched sound manifesting in my ears. I often think of it as an internal barometer, screaming out when I am not listening to my body. What I am not listening to is dependent on the day, but usually concerns diet, alcohol, not taking enough exercise, being too much in the mind or becoming overly stressed about a situation. So, we must re-frame how we view the illness, disease or condition.

Try meditating or journeying to ask your body why it is the way it is. Ask why you have the ailment or issue. What is it trying to tell you? To change diet, slow down, show more love, listen more, speak your truth, be more generous, exercise more, nurture yourself or all the above?! You could also try the *transmuting trauma* and *Ho'opono pono* exercises, visualising the disease as a mass sitting opposite you at the table.

As previously mentioned, if you are someone who spends a lot of time in your mind, try writing a letter to the illness. Start the letter with "Dear [ailment, i.e., fibromyalgia]", and tell the condition how it has affected you, influenced your life and impacted those around you. Let it know the pain you have felt and are still feeling. Put everything you can down on paper. Then write another letter from your ailment to you, starting with "Dear [your name]", and this time write with your non-normal hand. The words will be harder to write and therefore occupy your logical mind, freeing up your creative, more intuitive side, to be the voice of the ailment. Allow any emotions that come up to be released. Create a ceremony around this exercise to show your intention to be at peace with your condition, perhaps burning your letters afterwards as an act of letting go.

Another method is to visualise the illness or disease inside you, before using one of the letting go processes to transmute it and see it leaving your body. For example, visualise cancerous cells as dark blobs that can be washed away using one of the water exercises or a tumour broken apart when energetically pulled out using the *release using an object from nature* exercise. Visualise replacing what has been removed with healthy, vibrant cells and a colourful healing energy.

Other methods to work with ill health are to use powerful healing visualisations and rebuilding metaphors. Maybe see yourself as a castle with a few holes in the walls that need fixing or as a jigsaw with a couple of missing pieces. Repair your castle or complete your jigsaw. Additionally, you could visualise healing actions happening within you, such as seeing broken bones knit themselves together as a weave of woollen threads or visualising healthy cells multiplying, crowding out and vanquishing (or eating up) any diseased ones.

Talk yourself better by being positive and telling your body it is healed, and include an uplifting statement about having a healthy body in any affirmations you work with. However, be wary of washing over deep emotions by superficially covering yourself in a comfort blanket of positive thinking or false optimism.

For pain relief, try visualising the area as being calmed from an angry red to a peaceful blue or green, or the flame of pain being doused by a stream of water. See an intense pain as a tightened vice that you can ease off before seeing it fall away completely, or a clamped claw that you visualise releasing, maybe even watching the creature it belongs to fly away. Find a metaphor that works with you and the pain you feel.

After any spiritual work around letting go or the cleansing and removal of the unwanted, visualise yourself bathed in a healing light or colour, or a spiritual/divine energy, to fill any energetic gaps created by the release, sending love and healing to those parts of you that need it.

The West - Facing fears and death

"I could get right by myself. I could make it right, if i was brave enough, to listen to what was in my heart and do something about it."
Bhodi Rook, Rogue One.

The West section looks at facing your fears, feelings around death and living your life as well as you can. It is represented by Jaguar (a female jaguar) in the symbolism this book draws upon. A powerful animal stalking us through life, able to strike at any time from the shadows, but also a mother and protector, teaching us to bravely face life head-on. The exercises in this section can help answer some penetrating questions: what fears do you have? what fears have been inherited? what are your experiences around death and losing a loved one? what are your feelings about your own mortality? what are you doing to live life to the full now? are you living healthily? are you honouring the sacredness of the life you have been given? Plenty to ponder then over the coming pages.

Move out of your comfort zone

Something we haven't tried before or not experienced does not have to loom large over us and create fear. Even if we have trepidation with an activity, it is unlikely to be as bad as we think. Spending time out of your comfort zone can help dissolve fears of the new, the unfamiliar and the unknown. A few simple ideas to try include:

- Vary your walk to work or when running errands. Take another route, even if it may be longer.

- Visit somewhere new.

- Talk to a stranger. Do this each day for three days.

- Wear clothes or a colour you wouldn't normally wear.

- Try different foods.

- Change the way you automatically do something. For example, washing your hair, having a bath or making a meal. Try doing things differently, even if it feels slower or less effective.

- Try a new pastime or activity.

- Challenge yourself. When you give advice or offer an opinion, challenge yourself. Are you sure about what you said? Why did you feel the need to say it? Is there another perspective that you may not be seeing?

- Personal space. Personal boundaries are developed so that individuals feel comfortable when interacting with others. Social limits and cultural differences affect these distances, as do medical situations, e.g., social distancing during the coronavirus pandemic. Try blurring these lines a little, allowing others to come closer if they wish (as long as it is safe). Understand why you do not (or maybe do) like people coming closer.

Fears
Note: Safety warning

There are various ways to approach fears and understand any anxieties around them. The idea is not to overcome the fear, although that may be desired if it is affecting your life detrimentally, but to embrace it and, as the saying goes, "feel the fear and do it anyway." When facing a fear, the chemical rush – the buzz of adrenaline – is palpable and actively searched out by many to add to the spice of life. Watching horror movies, performing in front of a live audience, clambering through pitch-black cave systems or jumping out of a plane at 12,000 ft are all great examples. There may be apprehension and fear before the activity, but willpower overcomes any 'flight' response as we push ourselves onwards into and through the experience, knowing the rewards will be worthwhile.

However, there may be fears we do not consciously want to face and subconsciously go to great lengths to avoid: those beyond any obvious traumatic experience and perhaps rooted somewhere in childhood. Examples are:

- Being lost (e.g., in a crowd, shopping mall or forest)
- A fear inherited or *picked up* from a parent.
- Being bullied (by a sibling, someone at school, a child/adolescent living near you)
- Unsafe situations (in retrospect) around, for example, water, heights, confined spaces, crowds, loud noises, certain people.
- An unpleasant encounter with an animal (wild or domesticated), perhaps being startled by it.
- Scared by something you were told, read, watched on TV or saw on the internet.

Any negative experience in your life could be a root cause of a phobia, and it is worth adding any profound fear from this list to your *Life CV*, estimating when it first started or became apparent.

Exposure therapy is one of the most effective ways to treat a chronic phobia. It involves an experienced therapist coaching the individual to deal with their anxiety when approaching or "being exposed" to the object or situation they fear. This can be done gradually, over several sessions or in a single prolonged session, depending on the individual's readiness to progress. Fear of animals such as spiders, rats, pigeons, snakes, dogs and insects are common phobias that can be controlled and overcome with exposure therapy. But there are also actions you can take for yourself. Firstly, ask yourself if you recall when this fear first began. Is there a reason or a root cause, such as an incident with this animal in your childhood? Secondly, read a book about the animal, ideally one with pictures, and try to understand as much as you can about it: its evolution, natural behaviour and its place in nature. Watch documentaries about the animal, noting any remarkable or positive characteristics. Then move on to more tactile interaction. Paint or draw the animal, keep a photo of one with you and become familiar with it - even buy yourself a toy of the animal. Visit a pet shop or zoo to *meet* the animal, and try to become comfortable being near one in captivity.

All the above should help alleviate anxiety around the animal, but you can also carry out a shamanic journey to the spirit of the animal to unearth more information as to why you fear it. Maybe there is a hidden message from the animal for you, some wisdom you need to learn and incorporate into your life. See the section on shamanic journeying for more information on how to do this. If you are unsure of a spirit animal's meaning, search for it on the internet and see if the information given resonates.

Try testing yourself in small, totally safe ways for other types of fear. For example, if you fear heights, look at activities such as climbing the stairs in a tall building and looking out at each floor, noting how you feel. Or push a little further by walking across a high bridge, trying zip lining or tree-top canopy walking. If it is confined spaces, try spending time in small spaces that you can quickly leave, such as a shed, tiny room or cupboard. For fear of darkness, wear a blindfold for a period of time. Again, carry out a shamanic journey to uncover any deeper meaning to your anxiety, perhaps seeing what that fear represents metaphorically in your journey. Is it a person or situation from your living memory or maybe a past life manifesting in this life? How can you make peace with this fear? Additionally, I suggest that using one of the *letting go* exercises from the previous section would be helpful when dealing with a fear and its root cause. Of course, if you feel your anxiety or phobia is affecting your day-to-day life, obtaining professional help is highly recommended.

There are several other methods to go deeper into fear or anxiety and challenge yourself on a broader level, such as wearing flamboyant clothing that draws attention, speaking in public, singing in a choir, volunteering where you will come into contact with others less fortunate than yourself or even going as far as trying a firewalk.

Shadow self

We all have a shadow self. That part of us where our faults, inhibitions and fears reside – our personal demons. We all have them, as nobody is perfect, and nor should they be, for that matter. Life is not about being perfect or striving for perfection: be it in physical appearance, home and family life, relationships or achievements. Whomever you may know or read about in a magazine, seen on TV or the internet, and think they are perfect or have an ideal life, rest assured, they have their own issues and troubles going on one way or another. The key is not letting your negatively perceived reactions and behaviours control or define you. Accept you have a shadow self. Own it. Realise that it may come out now and again or seemingly control your actions at times, but also accept that it is there for your benefit and growth.

Listen to the script in your head to begin shedding light on your shadow self. What keeps repeating? What negative judgements do you have about people you know? What do you not like about them? Is there a trace of the trait within you? Life is often a mirror, so when we moan about someone or something, our feelings come from a place of reference and commonality within us. As the saying goes, "It takes one to know one." We can also expect too much from people, especially if we expect a lot from ourselves, possibly due to demanding or exacting parents. If such expectations are not met, a sense of lack or failure can result. Are your expectations of your own and other people's behaviour too high? Where in your life are you setting standards so elevated that failure is almost guaranteed?

List down your perceived negative traits, characteristics and behaviours. In the UK, we find it relatively easy to see the negative within ourselves rather than the positive, so don't be surprised at a long list if you are British! Against each negative trait, write down the opposite. Against this positive characteristic, list the times in your life when you have shown it. When completed, this list details the negative characteristics you believe you have, with their opposite positive characteristics, both of which you have felt and expressed. Hopefully, this should show that you are a far nicer and far better person than you perhaps thought you were.

The shadow self is a teacher. It has served you in the past, often as a way of protecting you. Your *loyal soldier*, as I heard it once said, fighting your corner. Do you still need them fighting so strongly for you? Try asking your *loyal soldier* to step back. Meditate or journey with it, thanking it for all the protection it has given you over your life, but now it is time for it to take a back seat.

Antagonist list

In a similar way to the *shadow self* exercise, think of a person from your life, who you believe has affected you detrimentally, and list down the negative traits you feel they possess or that they showed you, one below the other. Then across from each one, write the opposite positive trait. Do you think they have any of these good characteristics? Why did you see the negative? What do you think is stopping them from being the positive? Do you have any of these negative traits? The answers to these questions may show you that the judgements made about others may not be as clear-cut as first thought. Maybe they are reflecting back part of yourself, revealing more of your shadow self.

Mistakes

We have all made mistakes. They are part of learning and growing up. Mistakes come with the territory when trying something new, stepping outside of our comfort zone or working from a place of not knowing. Therefore, we can usually let them slide, especially if we have learnt any inherent lesson. However, some mistakes, made recently or in the past, may still carry guilt or shame, and an act of atonement felt necessary. If you think you have made such a mistake, for example, by wronging someone or not behaving as you should have, and a direct apology is not possible or appropriate, try one of the *letting go* exercises covered in the previous section. Alternatively, make a note of the pertinent mistakes and then jot down alongside each one the lesson hidden within.

You can also hold a ceremony to apologise to anyone you may have hurt, giving thanks for the lessons and letting go of any emotion attached. A simple ceremony is fine, lighting a candle, writing and burning a letter, using an object from nature or a simple prayer sitting at your altar. Take responsibility for your actions, even if you believe others were at fault or to blame. Owning the situation is different from accepting all the blame yourself. By working on and releasing any negative energies around the event, you not only help yourself but, in the global landscape of energetic interaction, you may be helping any others involved, even if the *how* is unclear to you.

Making mistakes when conducting spiritual work is fine too. Again, nobody is perfect. If you feel that you may have done something incorrectly or been disrespectful, stop and apologise, in your mind or out loud, before continuing. We are all children spiritually. All mistakes are forgivable, as there is not one spirit, ascended master, benevolent ancestral force, god or deity that would not forgive a child, especially if that child was trying to learn and grow.

Darkness

Darkness is where we come from, within the womb, without light. But it holds a primordial fear. As children, darkness can be where monsters await, the bogeyman's domain, the doorway to nightmares. It represents the unknown and a place where fear lurks. As we grow up, this fear of darkness will hopefully pass or be vastly diminished. But it is easy to see why such anxiety may perpetuate.

In reality, darkness accounts for a third of our lives – the time when we sleep. But sleep can be a little fraught and hard to come by for some people. For example, painful physical ailments and medical issues or worries about life's problems can all lead to restless sleep and long nights. Then, of course, there are our dreams and nightmares, in which we can conjure up disturbing imagery, relive a dreadful experience or encounter a general manifestation of our fears. All the above can make bedtime, night time and darkness a place that can hold fear for us. It is, however, the mind chatter that creates the fear and uneasiness, not the darkness. So it is worth befriending this blackness, for darkness should be welcomed as a friend and not feared as a foe.

Shamans, mystics and similar seekers have used darkness for centuries (even millennia) as a place of peace and refuge to explore and find insight. Chambers within the ground, such as natural caves or a burrow dug out of the earth, can give not only the dark space to *work* within but also provide a deeper connection to the planet, as they are physically within the earth – in the surrogate womb of Mother Earth if you will. Examples include ancient burial mounds, specific types of North American sweat lodge and the kivas of the Pueblo people. Where the ground is too hard to be excavated, man-made structures, such as temples and similar ceremonial buildings or above-ground sweat lodges and kivas, can be used for connection to the sacred while in darkness.

Finding a local natural cave to use is likely to be difficult, but you may be able to create your own *cave* by converting a room at home simply by blocking out all the light. This is probably impractical for most people, so wearing a blindfold is a good alternative. A blindfold will allow total darkness to be worked with, compared to simply closing your eyes, which allows some ambient light in, especially during the daytime. A blindfold also alleviates light from any automatic eye flutter and, if a Mindfold is used (which has cut-outs for the eyes), allows the wearer to stay in complete darkness even with eyes relaxed or half open.

Purposefully spending time in darkness can have several benefits. Firstly, it can help face any fears of being in the dark, possibly stemming from childhood. We all had nightmares of one sort or another when we were young, which can echo throughout our adult lives. Secondly, darkness is the place to go for meditation and visualisation. After a period in darkness, the lack of visual stimulus heightens our other senses and shifts our focus, slowing us down and moving us toward inner stillness and deeper connection. New feelings and sensations can come up to be explored and played with. Even just the sense of entering another world. Finally, going into darkness for spiritual work links you directly to those that have gone before. As mentioned, for millennia, many cultures across the planet have used darkness for spiritual experiences. By doing so yourself, you are joining a long line of seekers and connecting to the explorer energy within us all.

Even if we feel content in our life, there is always a questioning part of us (albeit possibly suppressed) that wants to know a little bit more, go somewhere new or try something different. Variety is, after all, the spice of life. So, even if just once for the experience, it is worth spending an extended time (while awake) in darkness.

Note: Safety warning
When we are in darkness, others automatically know to leave us alone: "Don't disturb her – she's sleeping/meditating/praying." If you sit on a park bench with your eyes closed, you will most likely not be disturbed. People know to leave you alone. Try it. At first, you will be aware of everyone passing by you, and you may feel that they are staring or about to disturb you. Let this pass and slowly sink deeper into the darkness. If you do this on a sunny day, notice the *colour* of the darkness you are in. If you look towards the Sun with your eyes closed, *see* the colours as they slowly change and immerse yourself in each. Reds, oranges, yellows, maybe some indigo and

purple, even colourful flashes. Of course, do not look directly at the Sun with open or even half-open eyes. You could permanently damage your eyesight.

A final point to make, on an evolutionary note, is that before the dinosaurs, there was a mass extinction event (science says there have been at least five such events in the Earth's history), that wiped out most species except for those living underground. It is highly likely our pre-dinosaur ancestors were burrowers and lived underground most of their lives. Perhaps our connection to the darkness is part of our genetic makeup, passed on through our DNA. Perhaps working with darkness reignites this part of our chemistry and is something we have evolved to work with. If not, why would the effects of working with darkness be so profound? Evolution tends only to keep what is necessary and what works.

Darkness exercises
Note: Safety warning

Below is a rough outline of an approximately two-hour session, including suggestions for exercises that can be carried out. Initially, or if you have some reservations about darkness, try immersing yourself for a few minutes to half an hour. Ideally, it is worth spending two to three hours in continual darkness.

Before beginning a long session, do all you can to ensure you will not be disturbed so your focus will be inward and without distraction. You will be moving around in darkness, so familiarise yourself with the space you will be in for the period. You may stay in one room or, as is more likely, you will be moving around your home. Prepare the space by clearing the area and removing anything breakable. Gather a few objects from your altar to work with, along with something wooden (i.e., your tapping stick) and a stone or crystal to represent *Mother Earth*. Have a blanket, some water to drink and some tissues handy (as emotions may be released). Ideally, also have a rattle or hand drum nearby, and prepare any music you will use. You may find it beneficial to have some gentle background music or a drumbeat playing, but this is a personal choice.

Create a space where you can lie down with everything you need within easy reach. Let's call this your ceremonial area. Firstly open space standing in the middle of your ceremonial area. Then go into darkness by putting on your blindfold. Spend some time acclimatising to the darkness and wandering around your space. Be conscious of slowing your movements down. Explore the room you are in. Touch things and get your bearings a little. Start by going a small distance and then returning to your ceremonial area. Then try going further. Be still often, simply listening. If you need the bathroom, try to stay in darkness while using the facilities.

While in your ceremonial area, work with each of the altar objects you have chosen. Try meditating with each or focusing upon one as you rattle or drum and carry out a journey with it. Or hold each one in turn and move around your area, *seeing* (in your mind) or feeling what comes up. If emotions arise, allow yourself to go entirely into them and release them where necessary. Tapping parts of your body with your stick or fingers can help with the release.

Once you feel you have completed the work with the objects, take a moment to give thanks for anything that has been released. Ensure you feel grounded again before continuing. Try any or all of the following:

- Practice yoga or any other gentle movement routine you are familiar with.

- Use a rattle or drum and gently move, sway or dance. Be aware of the space around you, being careful not to knock anything over. If you have prepared it, play some music and dance away with total abandon, again being conscious not to fall over or crash into anything.

- Try an energy visualisation. Imagine pulling in energy as a colour, ribbon of light or similar from above, down into your head, through your body and out into the ground. Reverse this, drawing energy up from the earth, through your body and out of your crown into the Universe. Play with this.

- If you are feeling adventurous, maybe go outside into a garden or outdoor private and safe space. I strongly warn against going out onto balconies or other high places as you will be in a disorientated state and liable to trip or topple over. Also, it is likely you will be experiencing heightened feelings, and the sense that you will want to fly could be quite overpowering. Do not go out into a public place or near traffic due to the obvious dangers.

Return to your ceremonial area and again take some time to give thanks, centre and ground yourself. Go back into silence and lay down, focussing your intention toward connecting to *Mother Earth*, ensuring your wooden object and stone or crystal are nearby. Take hold of the wooden object and visualise yourself in a wooded area connecting to the trees: their strong trunks, the branches reaching up to the sky, the roots going down into the earth. Meditate, journey or simply be with this visualisation. Spend time in this wooded area, feeling welcomed by the trees. Strengthen your connection to the tall standing ones by communicating with them and allowing a dialogue to flow. What do they want to say to you? What do you want to tell them? Play with this. Then take your stone or crystal and visualise yourself going deep into the earth and connecting with the rocks, maybe in a cave deep within the earth or in the heart of a mountain. Again, play with this through meditation or journeying, saying what you wish to say to the planet and hearing what the rocks and the energies deep within the Earth wish to communicate with you.

With both the wooden and stone or crystal objects, follow your intuition and allow your visualisation and the sensations felt to strengthen your connection to the Earth. Allow yourself to be transported throughout the natural world, visiting any natural place or meeting any animal you wish, or that the darkness wants to show you. At some point, ask *Mother Earth* what her greatest need is right now and what more you can do to help her. When finished, give thanks to *Mother Earth* for all she provides.

Other activities to try in darkness:

- Chant, recite a mantra or play with sound and your voice. Maybe find your own sound, a sound that resonates with you. (See *The North* chapter.)
- Listen to nature.
- Pray or meditate.
- Focus on your body. Touch, massage and caress yourself.
- Have a bath (safely!)
- Draw something or be creative in a simple way, using your other senses rather than sight.
- Eat something (made beforehand, easily prepared without sight or something prepared for you.) Focus on the smell, taste and texture. Notice how your eating automatically slows down when in darkness.

Please do not try to cook, boil water, make a fire or carry out any other potentially dangerous task.

Bring yourself back to your ceremonial area and, as a final exercise in darkness, try visualising or journeying to a cave or underground temple, and feel the presence of the ancestors in this place. It has seen a millennia of spiritual people, seekers and pilgrims immerse themselves in the darkness, connect to the planet and be given insight into their life journeys. Now you are here, exploring this liminal space. Connect to those that have gone before and spend some time in gratitude.

It is now time to thank the darkness and return to the light. Stand up in your ceremonial area and visualise roots coming from your feet. Spend a few moments bringing grounding energy into your body from the earth. Give thanks for your time spent in darkness and for any insights you may have been given before gently removing the blindfold. Ensure you feel grounded and close the space. Afterwards spend some time noting how you feel, maybe journalling any experiences and insights. Are there any issues or fears that were not suitably resolved? Be gentle with yourself for the rest of the day or evening.

Grief for a deceased loved one

> *"But what is grief, if not love persevering."*
> Vision, WanderVision.

Grief is a process. It is different for each person, and there should be no expectation on how we should grieve. We are, however, conditioned in the West to be somewhat reserved when it comes to grief, to hold things in and not show any emotion, as we are told this is a sign of weakness, for men in particular. But this attitude is unhealthy as being aware of and able to express our feelings is a sign of emotional maturity, and a strength in both men and women.

Emotions can sometimes get stuck or be locked away. Over time they can begin to fester. The more we bury them, the more impact they can have on us at a physical level. They are burdens we do not have to carry. If someone we love dies, someone we were close to, it hurts. It is painful. That person is no longer part of our daily world. No more sharing of good times, no more confiding in, no more helping or being helped, no more of their *energy* around, no more of their love to receive, and, just as sadly, they are no longer there to receive our love.

But we still have our memory of them. We can imagine or visualise them. So start by doing that. If there is someone you have lost, then begin by imagining them. See them at peace. If there were unresolved issues, things left unsaid before they left, then visualise saying these things to the person. Say whatever words come to you, whatever feels right, whether you believe they can hear you or not. It is for you to shift the emotion. Creating a virtual conversation allows you to go into and release the emotion. By releasing, I mean allowing yourself the space to cry, scream or curl up on the floor sobbing. Go wherever the emotion takes you. Try not to talk through any tears or hold back. This stops the process. If you need emotional support (or indeed physical), try holding onto something wooden, a staff or stick, for example, and feel the connection to something natural and to the Earth. If you want to help the visualising process, hold an object that belonged to your loved one or one that reminds you of them, while saying what you want to say. Tapping, with your fingers or a wooden stick, on your throat, chest and belly areas may be helpful as this can help shift energy.

Maybe go to a place that reminds you of them and give a (biodegradable) offering, saying some words or a prayer while there, or write a letter to your loved one and burn or post it, being mindful not to include full names or addresses. If drawn to, carry out one of the *letting go* exercises from *The South* section if you cannot go into the emotion as deeply as you would like, or try holding a memorial service for your beloved. This will give you time and space to go fully into any emotion, respectfully and privately. See the next section for a general outline.

When we are with someone suffering from grief, as much as we may want to, it is best not to comfort them if they are in a state of release, as this stops their grief process. We want to reach out and ease the pain they are clearly going through and, in turn, reduce the pain we are empathetically feeling, but this deprives the other person of a chance to go fully into their own process. In a public funeral situation, it is natural to hold and comfort those grieving. It would seem inhumane not to. In truth, to go completely into the emotion, it needs to be faced alone, head-on and without any shame or embarrassment.

How to conduct a memorial service for a loved one

> *"We've cried long enough. Let's do something that lets us love, respect and honour them without being morbid all the time."*
> Said in 1996 by Viola Parker, wife of Sergeant Earl Parker,
> killed in action over fifty years previously on D-Day 1944.[11]

In Western society, there is an organised funeral immediately or relatively quickly after the death of a loved one. This is often too soon for most people to work through their grief, especially if the

---

[11] From *The Bedford Boys* by Alex Kershaw, 2004, De Capo Press.

death was sudden. The funeral serves a purpose, of course, but the immediacy of its occurrence, the formalised ritual, any religious influence and the relatively impersonal nature of the ceremony may not feel right for truly expressing one's grief.

Holding a separate, deeply personal memorial service (or passing-over ceremony) for someone you love makes it far more applicable to you and your relationship with the person. Such a ceremony provides a space where the grief process can be entered into more fully without your guard up or, as is often the case in the UK, with a *stiff upper lip* and keeping the emotions under check, especially in the case of men. Some people may feel they never grieved properly for a loved one. Maybe they didn't want to express their emotions at the time, did not have a chance to grieve fully for one reason or another or felt they had to be strong for the rest of the family.

The circumstances surrounding the passing of a loved one also have a significant impact on how our emotions manifest. The shock of a sudden or unexpected death, a suicide, homicide or tragic accident can mean the grief process is almost bypassed and the emotions not given a chance to be accessed, let alone expressed. Of course, even the passing of someone naturally from old age can still be difficult and surrounded by grief.

Then there are global issues, such as the coronavirus pandemic that began in 2020. Covid-19 affected everyone and has taken (and continues to take) many lives, in some instances very quickly, often with the patient allowed limited contact with family and friends towards the end of their life. Additionally, and understandably, to minimise transmission of the virus, the number of funeral attendees was restricted in the UK (as in most countries), depriving people of being able to pay their respects in person. Even if people could attend, there were probably still specific Covid guidelines to follow and an underlying concern about being around others in a group situation, however slim the chance of infection, thus further distracting the attendees from being fully present in the ceremony.

Other large-scale losses such as disease, war, famine, genocide, ethnic and religious cleansing, natural disasters, etc., all lead to the loss of lives in devastatingly traumatic ways. All loss of life is hard to take. But when it seems senseless or of no fault of the deceased – based on circumstance, colour of skin, sexual orientation, faith or simply bad luck – there is inherent disbelief, a lack of comprehension and understandable anger at what has happened. All of which overshadow and undermine the grief process of those in mourning.

Conducting a memorial service can offer great solace for all and any circumstances around the loss of a loved one. There is no time frame for holding such a memorial. It can be relatively soon after the formal funeral or years, even decades, after your loved one has passed. The service can be either individual or with a group, but I suggest trying the individual ceremony first to familiarise yourself with the process and give yourself the opportunity to tap into your own grief, allowing the release and the expressing of any emotion. In both cases, the ceremony is conducted predominately for the people present, not the deceased. By that, I mean the ceremony is for those present to go fully and openly into the depth of their grief. It is not meant to be a celebration of the deceased's life. This can be done at another time in another ceremony. If the deceased was religious or had certain beliefs to be honoured then, by all means, incorporate them in some way but do not feel that the ceremony has to be led by these beliefs.

As individuals, perhaps we feel uneasy or unqualified to conduct a memorial service for a loved one, thinking that we may get it wrong or be disrespectful, especially when there is such a well-established industry around funerals. There is, however, no reason why you cannot hold your own ceremony for a loved one in any way you see fit, but I strongly advise that it should consist of a beginning, a middle and an end. Ending a ceremony is especially important psychologically, as this draws a line under proceedings and formally concludes the ceremony, thereby providing a sense of closure. Below is a suggestion that you may wish to use. Both the individual and group memorial services follow a similar outline.

- Prepare the area ready for the ceremony.
- Open the space.
- Conduct the memorial service.
- Close the space.
- Give thanks and ensure everyone present is grounded.
- Clear the area of personal items.

As a note, conducting such a ceremony doesn't mean that you have to let their memory go totally or are saying goodbye forever, let alone be free of the emotions or feelings you have for your loved one. The pain may well endure, the grief still present, but it is my hope (and experience) that you will be lighter and more comfortable in your own feelings, knowing that you have held a sacred ceremony based upon your love for the deceased. Of course, your loved one will not be forgotten and will forever live on in your memory.

Individual ceremony

The ceremony described here has its roots in the natural world and my shamanic training. As far as I know, it is not an appropriated sacred ceremony. As every culture and society has its own take on preparing a loved one for whatever lies beyond this life, there is no right or wrong way to carry out such a ceremony. There is also no need for any religious or spiritual beliefs to conduct such a ceremony. Intention, respect and love are all that matter.

Plan and prepare for your ceremony. Pick a time and day, and choose a suitable space for the ceremony. Ideally, a private space and one where you feel comfortable releasing any emotion. Either indoors or outdoors is okay. The dress code is entirely up to you. Dress up if you like, wear black or be casual. Whatever you feel comfortable wearing is OK. Collect together a few of your loved one's personal items, such as clothing, shoes, jewellery, etc., along with one photograph. The following may seem a little macabre, but I suggest positioning their possessions as if the deceased were lying down. Use a rolled-up blanket, pillows or cushions covered with a sheet or similar to represent the body and adorn it with their clothes. Place shoes at one end, jewellery where it would usually be worn and put the photograph near the head area. An actual photograph or one on a phone or tablet is fine. If you do not have any personal items, lay a sheet over the rolled-up blanket, pillows or cushions, and place a surrogate pair of shoes at one end and the photograph at the other. There's no need to go into too much detail here, just enough to evoke the sense that their body is in the room.

Don't forget a glass of water and a box of tissues. It's worth preparing for some emotion to come up, and in doing so, you are subconsciously telling yourself that shedding tears is OK. In fact, during this preparation process, you will probably feel very emotional anyway. Go into the emotion as it comes up. Cry. Release. You don't have to *save up* the emotion for the ceremony itself. This whole process is for you to go as fully as possible into your grief, allowing emotion to come up and be released whenever and however it manifests. In a way, this process started as soon as you decided to conduct the ceremony.

Before you begin the ceremony, open sacred space. You should be familiar with opening space from the previous exercises, but I shall reiterate the process here as a reminder. Opening space marks the beginning of the service, recognising the space as being ceremonial (for the duration of the ceremony), and is a way to say, "I am here, and I am ready to hold this ceremony for my loved one." However you wish to open space is fine, as it is the intention that counts. Some suggestions are to either say an opening prayer, invite the spirit of your loved one to be present, call to the directions (north, south, east, west, below and above), connect with God, Goddess, angels, spiritual leaders or spirit animals, or ask for ancestors and other loved ones in spirit to come and be with you.

There is no right or wrong here, or a necessity for any belief in the afterlife to do this. It is the intention that holds the power, not the reality of the situation. The intention is to invite those unseen (and energies unseen) to be present with you at this ceremony and comes only from a place of love. You are asking for help shifting the emotions of this life, the powerful feelings surrounding the loss and passing over of a loved one. It should feel both respectful and comforting. At no time should there be a fear of ghosts or anything supernatural. Only ever love.

Alternatively, offer up a humble request to the Universe, or for that outside of your consciousness (maybe your subconscious), to be present with you today for this ceremony. Allow any wording to come from the heart. Whatever words you use will be fine, as it is the intention that matters. If you are unsure, prepare something to say beforehand. Even though you are conducting this ceremony alone, try to say the words out loud and not only in your head. Burn some incense, smudge (the wafting of smoke from smouldering sacred plants or wood) or light a candle if you are drawn to. Play background music if you wish. Create an atmosphere that feels right for you.

So, you have prepared the space, set the scene and asked for help from whatever lies outside of your consciousness. Now is the time for the main body of the ceremony and for you to speak from the heart about your loved one. Speak your words as if they can hear you. Say what you want to say to them. Maybe say things that were not said when they were alive. Clear the air, get everything off your chest. Speak as if you were having a conversation with them, with their spirit. Pretending they are there or listening, whether you believe they can hear or not, psychologically brings you closer to them, thus creating a more personal and authentic ceremony. Talk freely with them and chat about whatever comes up. Even seemingly banal things if they come to mind. There is no need to rush, so spend as long as you want with this. Accept it will be a one-way conversation, but be open to signs of a response, an acknowledgement from the Universe for your humble ceremony. Maybe seeing a specific bird or animal in your garden, hearing a certain noise, or even seeing a particular image or programme on TV or the internet later that day. Do not get caught up in a two-way dialogue unless you are comfortable with your psychic abilities.

If you feel like you want to cry, sob, wail or collapse, do so. This is the chance for a release of emotion and the clearing of any emotional blockage. Feelings of embarrassment may surface by this show of emotion, but as you are conducting the ceremony alone and in private where nobody else can see or hear you, these feelings should pass quickly. Be brave. Go as deep as you can. Tap the throat, heart or belly areas with your fingertips or your short wooden stick to aid the release. You can also try drumming or rattling (a steady medium-paced beat) to give a background pulse to help occupy your mind and drive the release. If you don't have a hand drum or rattle, there are audio files or videos online that can be used instead. Having a wooden staff or walking stick for support and grounding is also helpful as it is something natural to hold, giving a solid connection to the earth.

Many emotions can come up, and perhaps not only around the person you are holding the ceremony for. Others who have died may come to mind, as may a pet or beloved animal, and you may release emotion around their passing. There may be emotions around broader issues such as the coronavirus pandemic, habitat loss, declining species numbers and extinctions, pollution, disease, war, famine, natural disasters, etc. Allow whatever that wants to come up to be expressed and released.

When you feel you have released as much as possible, tell your loved one that it is time to send them on their way. At this point, you may want to drum or rattle and visualise their spirit being taken away into the ether. Maybe chant or sing, and say "goodbye", "thank you", "I love you", or any other parting words you wish; words to help send them on their journey beyond this life. There is no right or wrong here. If it comes from the heart, then it is right. Feel as though you are helping them on their way, letting them go to wherever and whatever lies beyond.

This intention of sending them on their way reinforces any similar soul flight that may have occurred since their death. Even if you (or the deceased) have no belief in an afterlife, speaking out loud helps shift the emotions, more so than only thinking the sentiment. The act of sending them on their way as best you can is a potent symbol of your love. It can often provide some level of closure. As a suggestion, try using an eagle (or similar bird of prey) in your visualisation of their spirit or soul moving on. Visualise the eagle flying down and lifting your loved one up and away into the sky, reuniting them with the Universe/God/Great Spirit. Do your best to set them free and let them go a little more in your heart.

When you feel ready, close the space, signifying the end of the ceremony. Thank those unseen that you invited when you opened the space for coming and being present with you throughout the ceremony, whether you felt their presence or not. If you called in the directions, turn to face each one and give thanks. Give a final thank you to your loved one, knowing that you have done your best in sending them on their way spiritually. Spend a few moments in gratitude for what has transpired and feel proud that you have completed a beautiful ceremony honouring your beloved.

Afterwards, ensure you feel grounded and back in the present moment. As a reminder, a simple way to do this is to imagine roots coming from the bottom of your feet into the earth and connecting you to the planet. Feel balanced. If you have one, hold a wooden staff or stick, and feel the direct connection down through the wood into the earth. Having something to eat and drink or going for a walk in nature are also good ways to ground yourself.

As soon as possible after the ceremony and when you feel able to, clear up the area where you have been conducting the memorial, removing all the items. Try and do this with a lighter heart and a feeling of gratitude. Be careful not to create a shrine, as this is *holding on* rather than *letting go*.

If, on reflection, you feel there was more to be said or that you didn't do something correctly, you can always try writing a heartfelt letter to the deceased and posting it to the Universe or burning it ceremonially. Alternatively, hold another memorial service at a later date. That said, if the intention was there, one ceremony should be enough, even if it was not exactly how you wanted it. Undoubtedly it was as it should have been.

Group ceremony

Before holding a memorial service with other people present, I strongly advise conducting one on your own, to familiarise yourself with the process and provide the opportunity to tap into your own grief. When the individual ceremony has been completed, choose an appropriate date for the group ceremony and invite those you wish to attend. Inform them of the general outline of the service, asking them to bring one object that reminds them of the deceased. Also, advise them on what to wear. People often default to black, but whatever people feel comfortable wearing to such an event should be fine.

On the day of the service, prepare the space where you will conduct the ceremony. Use the rolled-up blanket or similar to represent the body and place the objects and photograph appropriately. Keep one particular item for the ceremony itself. Have water and tissues handy. When all your guests arrive, make them as comfortable as possible with what is about to happen. When conducting a ceremony, it is hard to please everyone due to their various beliefs, but all that matters is the intention and an open heart. Let them know this is a safe and loving space to show and release their emotions.

Open the space as you choose. The same method used in the individual ceremony is okay. Smudge or burn incense and light a candle. Play some background music, but remember this is not a celebration of the deceased's life. This ceremony provides a space for those present to release, let go and move through the grief process. So any music should be soft, soothing and maybe even sad. This is a space to go into the sadness and grief to release it, not to mask or avoid it. As with the individual ceremony, invite God, Great Spirit, ancestors, the directions, etc., to be present. Whatever feels suitable for the group is fine.

Show those present what to do by starting the process yourself. Place the object you have kept back on the representation of the body and speak your words to your beloved. Talk from the heart. Then invite each person, in turn, to come to the body, place down the object they have brought and say what they have to say, speaking as if the deceased were in the room. Give everyone time to say as much as they wish and allow them the space to release. I suggest that if anyone begins crying, wailing or even collapses on the floor, allow them the space to do this without consolation.

It is only natural that we want to console someone grieving and clearly in emotional pain. We want their pain to stop. We don't like how their pain makes us feel as it holds up a mirror to the grief we may be struggling to release from our hearts. But, by going to them, holding them or comforting them only acts to interrupt and stop their grief process. If you feel you must do something, tell them they are being extremely brave and now is the time to go deeply into the grief. Often one person's courage to lay bare their emotions can be a trigger for others present to do the same. One person's crying gives another permission to cry. So expressing these emotions is both cathartic and helpful to the group. Only if deep emotional releasing is prolonged and becomes too much should anyone be helped and comforted. You have to be the judge of this. Drumming or rattling with a repetitive beat can distract people's minds and help with grounding during and after the sharing and releasing.

Once all present have had time to speak, give everyone a final chance to say something. Often, by being in the ceremonial energy and witnessing family members or friends open up, others can become confident to speak freely and from the heart.

Conclude the ceremony by singing or chanting, sending the energy or spirit of the deceased on their way and saying goodbye. Keep any chant or song short and repetitive so everyone can join in easily. Ideally, do not use words, as these convey a specific meaning and not everyone's interpretation will be the same. Try singing or chanting from the heart and see what notes come out. As with the individual ceremony, ask those present to visualise the spirit of the deceased being taken away to the heavens, maybe by an eagle, to be reunited with the Universe, the ancestors, Great Spirit or God.

Allow the energies of the ceremony to settle with a few seconds of quiet contemplation.

Give thanks to those present for coming and being open to what has just happened, and to feel proud for being part of a beautiful ceremony honouring the deceased. Close the space and thank those unseen, be they ancestors, Great Spirit, God or the Universe for being with you today. Encourage everyone to ground themselves, imagining roots coming from their feet and going deep into the earth while taking a few balancing deep breaths.

Once the ceremony is formally closed, it is a good idea to share some food and drink, gather around a real fire or go for a walk together so everyone can chat, relax and feel more grounded.

When ready, clear the room and remove all the items and possessions as the ceremony is now over, and return the items brought to their owners. Do not leave the objects in place to become a shrine. Giving away your loved one's possessions, perhaps saving only a few keepsakes, is cathartic and can be done when the time feels right. Love is about letting go, not holding on.

The loss of a baby or child

Losing a child is painful, whatever the circumstances, and the grief felt must be unimaginable to those who have not been through such a traumatic event. Some comfort may be found in conducting an individual memorial or passing-over ceremony. Of course, there is likely to be a broader range of emotions felt, such as a deeper sense of injustice, a more pronounced feeling of loss, tremendous guilt (whatever the circumstances of the death), acrimonious blame or the shattering thought of a life not lived. It is also not the normal order of things. A child should outlive their parents.

I would suggest that any memorial is carried out with both parents present instead of individually, as this allows each parent to be there for one another and to understand more of the other's perspective, as the mother and father may differ in their grief and how they show it. Then, if wanted, a larger ceremony can be undertaken with more family members. To represent the child, use something small (maybe a doll or teddy bear) wrapped in a blanket. Again use a photo and place any sentimental objects on or near the blanket. Carry out the memorial in a similar way to the individual or group ceremony outlined previously, again with the primary intention of working through the grief from such a tragic loss.

Losing a child through abortion or miscarriage is clearly also traumatic, particularly for the mother, who may have had to face the tragedy in private, possibly even alone. There is no reason a memorial service cannot be held for this loss, conducted similarly to the loss of a child ceremony, using a small doll/teddy (or whatever feels right for you) wrapped in a blanket to represent the unborn life. Also, I suggest not giving a name to the child if it was never met in life, as parents may change their minds on a name once the child is born. This is, however, a personal choice.

Gravestones, memorials and the scattering of ashes

The use of a gravestone, memorial plaque, planting of a tree or any other way of remembering and honouring your loved one are all personal and entirely down to the individual and family wishes. However, I would say that it is best to avoid forming a shrine to the deceased, which is often the case when it comes to the loss of a baby or child. Many small graves in cemeteries are elaborately decorated and adorned with children's toys, playthings and photographs. Clearly, any comfort the parents and family can take by tending the grave is paramount, but be careful not to let it become a shrine over time. How much time is enough is up to the individual, and each parent or family will be different, especially when there is peer or family pressure, guilt or shame.

Scattering ashes is personal and can be carried out however you see fit. By all means, create a ceremony around the process, but saying a few words or even simply being in a loving state of remembrance when you scatter the ashes is enough to honour your beloved.

Letting someone go (whatever their age) with love is to set them free. Holding their memory in your heart is enough but conducting a memorial service or passing-over ceremony, as outlined previously, can be cathartic and help those affected move on.

The afterlife

Currently, from a scientific point of view, nobody can confirm or deny the existence of an afterlife, although psychics, mediums and many spiritual or religious people are convinced of it. It is worth being open-minded because, as with many unknowns, perhaps one day the scientific community will be able to observe, measure and explain certain spiritual phenomena, giving credence to long-held beliefs of something beyond this life. That day maybe a year, twenty or five hundred from now, so, in the meantime, we have to rely on our own experiences and intuition, and decide for ourselves.

Something to be aware of is that many people have reported similar experiences towards the end of their lives, as in the cases of near-death experiences (NDEs). Dr Penny Sartori, was awarded a PhD for her research into NDEs in 2005, based on seventeen years working as an intensive care nurse in the UK, and has written several books on the subject. The below extract from an article by Brian McIver for the Daily Record[12] explains more:

"Over a four year period Dr Sartori spoke to patients who had actually died, after a cardiac arrest where their heart stopped beating. She found out that seventeen percent had a NDE.

'They are all unique, but they do tend to follow a pattern. Some report travelling through a tunnel towards the light, and feeling magnetically drawn to the light. Once in the light, they find a beautiful landscape with lush green grass and beautiful flowers.

They often meet deceased relatives, and sometimes a being of light or religious figure, who are usually associated with the

---

[12] Brian McIver, article *Ex-nurse Dr Penny Sartori studies amazing experiences of people who come back from the dead*, Daily Record, 25/01/11.

person's own religion or culture. Very often, they have a conversation with the relatives or the being of light, who tells them to go back, it's not their time. Others will have a life review, where they will watch their whole life pass before their eyes or have an out-of-body experience, where they view their own emergency situation from above.'

In the thirteen years Dr Sartori has been studying NDEs, she has heard some incredible accounts.

'One man had a very clear out-of body experience, which I had published in a journal. He very accurately described my and the doctor's actions caring for him, at the time he was deeply unconscious. He gave a very accurate account of what had happened, and also described going into a pink room, where his dead mother and a Jesus type figure told him it wasn't his time and he had to go back. He was sixty and had suffered all his life from cerebral palsy. From birth, his right hand was in a contracted position but, following his experience, he was able to open up his hand. There was no medical explanation for that at all. There are other cases where people have been healed, but all we know is there is something going on that we can't explain.

When I started, everyone thought it was a bit of a joke and made fun of me. But as it progressed and more research came out, more people started to take notice and doctors are becoming more open-minded and more aware of it. The most important part is the idea of consciousness, where it begins and where it ends. These experiences have given us different ideas of what we currently believe consciousness to be, so we have to keep an open mind, and a lot more research is needed. I am a lot more open-minded. We need to do a lot more research and look at things differently. Science says consciousness is created by the brain, but maybe is just mediated by the brain. Through studying death, what it has really taught me is more about life, and how precious it is.'"

Dying impeccably

Death and the thought of death are somewhat taboo subjects in many modern Western cultures, even though we know we are all going to die. The fears around death can be diminished if you take the time to focus on it and, to some extent, prepare for it. If your time was up, if a giant asteroid was going to hit the Earth tomorrow, annihilating everything, what regrets would you have about your life and how you lived it? What would you want to do with your last 24 hours alive? What has previously stopped you from doing these things? Has anything been left unsaid or unresolved? Who do you need to forgive? Who do you need to apologise to? If speaking to these people is difficult or impossible, try writing them a letter and either post it to the Universe or ceremonially burn it.

Bronnie Ware is an Australian nurse who spent several years working in palliative care, caring for patients in the last twelve weeks of their lives. She recorded their dying epiphanies and put her observations into a book, *The Top Five Regrets of the Dying*[13], summarised below:

"1. *I wish I'd had the courage to live a life true to myself, not the life others expected of me.*
This was the most common regret of all. When people realise their life is almost over and look back clearly on it, it is easy to see how many dreams have gone unfulfilled. Most people had

[13] Bronnie Ware, *The Top Five Regrets of the Dying, 2012, Hay House.*

not honoured even a half of their dreams and had to die knowing that it was due to choices they had made or not made. Health brings a freedom very few realise, until they no longer have it.

2. *I wish I hadn't worked so hard.*
This came from every male patient that I nursed. They missed their children's youth and their partner's companionship. Women also spoke of this regret, but as most were from an older generation, many of the female patients had not been breadwinners. All of the men I nursed deeply regretted spending so much of their lives on the treadmill of a work existence.

3. *I wish I'd had the courage to express my feelings.*
Many people suppressed their feelings in order to keep peace with others. As a result, they settled for a mediocre existence and never became who they were truly capable of becoming. Many developed illnesses relating to the bitterness and resentment they carried as a result.

4. *I wish I had stayed in touch with my friends.*
Often they would not truly realise the full benefits of old friends until their dying weeks and it was not always possible to track them down. Many had become so caught up in their own lives that they had let golden friendships slip by over the years. There were many deep regrets about not giving friendships the time and effort that they deserved. Everyone misses their friends when they are dying.

5. *I wish that I had let myself be happier.*
This is a surprisingly common one. Many did not realise until the end that happiness is a choice. They had stayed stuck in old

patterns and habits. The so-called 'comfort' of familiarity overflowed into their emotions, as well as their physical lives. Fear of change had them pretending to others, and to themselves, that they were content, when deep within, they longed to laugh properly and have silliness in their life again."

Death is inevitable, but doesn't have to be the unspoken cloud that looms on the horizon. It should be openly honoured as the transition it is. In many cultures, death and the passing of a loved one are ritualised and celebrated with ceremonies and festivals. The Day of the Dead in Mexico is an annual festival that honours the deceased, and a time when families gather and pay their respects in remembrance and celebration rather than in sadness and regret.

While travelling with friends many years ago, we visited Tana Toraja, on the island of Sulawesi, Indonesia. We came across a festival in full flow, with music, food and drink, and rodeo-like activities happening in a central arena. We inquired as to the reason for this gathering, and were told it was another day in a six-month funeral for one of the local community elders, who had passed a number of years ago. The family had spent the interim years saving up enough money to afford such a festival, so their loved one could be sent on their way in the fashion their status demanded in the Toraja culture.

Such cultures, where death is an accepted part of life, diffuse the fear around it, as the community is familiar with it. This familiarity is made all the more poignant when the family and local community deal with the deceased and the funeral themselves. In the UK, we defer to others regarding the final moments of life and our subsequent passing. Towards the end, we are told what to do by unfamiliar doctors and nurses, hospital or hospice staff. After death, our body is handed over to another set of strangers for cremation or burial, often with a relatively impersonal ceremony.

An open casket wake may seem macabre to our standoffish point of view, but this offers several opportunities to diminish the stigma around death. Firstly, it allows those attending to see a dead body, perhaps for the first time, thus building up a familiarity with death. Secondly, this is a chance to see a loved one at peace and (usually) in their own home, where we knew them to be happy and content, rather than the last place they were alive, be that a hospital or hospice – both impersonal places of suffering, however caring and professional the staff are. Finally, it offers a chance to say goodbye to the deceased, perhaps in a similar way as described earlier, in the section *How to conduct a memorial service for a loved one.*

A final point on dying is about being able to exercise some control around your death. This includes planning for your passing, ensuring your affairs are in order, any regrets or unsaid words are dealt with and any funeral arrangements planned and provided for. Additionally, ensure procedures or systems are in place to help with any foreseeable problems with your passing, and you have enough pain relief, clothing and equipment available to be as comfortable as possible towards the end. Any medical professionals or spiritual counsellors should be aligned with your wishes and ensure that you are made aware of anything that may happen to you, including physical changes and possible symptoms or side effects of medication. Such foresight is one thing if we are facing a long-term illness, but the occurrence of a sudden or swift passing must also be considered. We never know when our time is up, so it is prudent to take some time out to face our mortality and become a little more familiar with the ending of our lives.

Living impeccably

If we are going to think about dying impeccably, then surely we should consciously try to live impeccably. This may seem like a high ideal, but it does not mean being perfect. It means honouring and being true to yourself, your emotions and feelings, and caring for your mind and body. Taking steps to look at all areas of your life from a healthy lifestyle perspective is worthwhile, remembering to be gentle with yourself and to make changes gradually. Exercise, good sleep patterns, positive relationships, social activities and taking time for yourself are all known to have benefits.

One of the most significant impacts on our health is the food we consume. Dietary choices are evidently important, with the gut microbiome's effect on overall health becoming increasingly accepted as a key factor. A varied healthy diet to nourish the human body and the non-human microbes, especially those in the gut, can help the fight against illness by boosting the immune system and other bodily defence systems. However, affecting and changing the gut microbiome bacterial flora is a personalised science. Each person's gut is different, so the development of a dietary plan has to be tailored to the individual. A particular food item, even if labelled a superfood, does not necessarily mean it will be helpful for all those who eat it.

Additionally, our diet is very different from our ancestors, especially since the advent of large-scale farming and processed foods. The increased use of fertilisers, pesticides and chemicals, married with the use of preservatives and artificial flavourings in production, have changed the food we eat beyond what our grandparents would recognise, let alone what those cultures that live directly off the land would know as food. Pollutants have also found their way into the food chain and are now ingested by us daily. Therefore, the food and drink we consume are as important to our health and mental wellbeing as any other facet of our lives.

Living impeccably also calls upon us to find ways to live as richly and harmoniously as possible and to pursue happiness, but not for the sake of all other aspects of life. Philosophy, both ancient and modern, points us towards a considered life; to contemplate upon and engage with life. This will be discussed later in *The Centre* chapter.

The North - Seeing the magic and joy in life, and connecting with the ancestors

> *"It has taken an eternity to make us yet*
> *our life spans are brief."*
> Buddhist monk.

The North is represented by Hummingbird and is the direction in which we honour those that have gone before and realise that wonder, magic and joy are a part of life, even if we sometimes lose sight of this. The hummingbird is a magical creature. How can she fly as she does? The speed of her wing beat, her aerodynamics and manoeuvrability. She puts on an aeronautical display, flitting from flower to flower in her search for nectar, moving forwards, backwards and sideways at will. Metaphorically, this shows we do not always have to move in the same direction to make headway on our life path. Hummingbird's diminutive size masks the ferocity with which she defends her territory and nest. Small does not mean weak. Determination, doggedness and courage are attributes hummingbird reflects back to us. How determined are we to achieve what we want in our lives? What is our epic journey? We have much to be thankful for and, whatever our upbringing, we have survived and are at the forefront of human evolution. Our ancestors had different opinions, beliefs and behaviours. Their world and culture were different from ours, but there are similarities. What can we learn from them? What do we need to remember?

Paths to happiness

There are many simple actions you can take to boost your happiness, such as:

- Smile
- Foster relationships
- Move and dance
- Laugh or watch comedy
- Be active
- Meditate
- Listen to music
- Give yourself a treat
- Recall past positive experiences
- Perform acts of kindness
- Clean something
- Repair something
- Cook a wholesome meal
- Practice mindfulness
- Express gratitude
- Practice forgiveness
- Create purpose in your life
- Be creative
- Go outside and be in nature
- Stroke a pet or friendly animal
- Caress yourself
- Love and be loved.

Connection and the senses

We are in a constant state of connection. Firstly, our biology and physiology connect us genetically to our ancestors and, if we go back far enough, to the last universal common ancestor (estimated to be 3.5 billion years ago) and subsequently to all life on this planet. That is quite a link and one easily dismissed, especially when we look at the diversity of life on Earth. It is true (but possibly difficult to accept) that we share 85% of our DNA with mice or, more astoundingly, 50-60% with bananas![14]

We are also connected to the world around us. Connected to it by our senses, giving us instant feedback about our environment and how we are experiencing it. Remove one of the senses and we immediately feel a partial loss of connection. However, over time this can be overcome by a subsequent increase in sensitivity of one or more of the remaining senses as the brain rewires synapses to compensate. Daniel Kish, President of World Access for the Blind, is a completely blind man from California who *sees* the world by using vocal clicks as a form of echolocation. His hearing and the parts of his brain used to process sound, have been adapted to allow him to interpret the reflected clicks into a mental map of the environment. He describes the world in front of him as composed of textures, rather than the visual description a normally sighted person would give, and is comfortable and skilled in navigating this way.

In a physically impaired situation like Daniel's, this compensation by the brain and the other senses happens automatically. This can be simulated, to a degree, by artificially removing one of your senses, e.g., by wearing a blindfold for an extended period. There will be a noticeable change in your other senses and perhaps the realisation that the world can be perceived differently, as highlighted in the *darkness* exercises from *The West* chapter.

---

[14] *Do People and Bananas Really Share 50 Percent of the Same DNA?* HowStuffWorks website. Alia Hoyt, updated Apr 2021.

Tuning into the senses, giving each one a little more focus now and again, can help with our connection to the world and our place within it, especially if we sometimes harbour feelings of separation. Strengthening our connection improves our sense of belonging and can, in turn, aid mental health. Belonging to something, being part of a group, a member of the team, being a supporter, a follower, a disciple or worshipper, all reinforce this sense of belonging. Ultimately this can evoke within us a feeling of *home*. Not in a bricks-and-mortar way, but rather as a sense inside that we are where we belong, in a place of connection and shared values. If you go into nature and actively sense and cultivate this connection to all that is around you; to the plants, trees, animals, rocks and stones; to the mountains, rivers, oceans, clouds, wind and rain; to the Sun, Moon and stars, you will be tapping into the same feelings, the same emotions and deep set awe that many, both today and throughout history, have tapped into: a sense of belonging, connection and an intrinsic ability to feel the energy of life. You are never alone in nature.

Conversely, city life can wear these connections down, even cut them, leading to a degree of loss (some would say a soul loss); losing the part of you that is not used, diminished or disconnected. Fortunately, even though this can feel like a loss, it can be reversed, brought back and reinstalled, simply by spending time in nature.

The senses and how to work with them is a vast subject with countless books, courses and therapies devoted to each. Notably, the senses work together, so while one may seem dominant, the others still have a role to play. The obvious example is food, where it is not only taste that is important to our eating experience but also how the food looks, its smell, texture and even the sounds made as we chew. A few ideas are touched upon here, but if you are drawn to one in particular, try to explore it further.

Sound: e.g., vibration, resonance, sounds of nature, drumming, music, singing, cymatics (the geometric patterns sound creates in liquids), chanting, tinnitus, sound healing, ASMR[15], silence.

Sounds are used to great effect on TV and in movies, e.g., in the film Star Wars, the robotic droid R2D2 does not speak English but communicates with electronic chirps and beeps, from which it is easy to understand the context of what it is trying to say. A couple more good examples of sounds precisely communicating a feeling, this time from TV, are Pingu's squeaks and squawks, and the Teletubbies' gibberish. Of course, these programmes are aimed at children, but as all parents know, when communicating with an infant or toddler, non-linguistic sounds are natural.

How noisy is the place where you are? Notice the sounds around you. How many are natural? How many are man-made? Which sounds are peaceful to you?

Sight: e.g., light, darkness, colours, shapes, mandalas, art, the natural world, imagery created in the mind, colour therapy.

Actively seek out nature to interact with and gaze upon. In a city, try wandering through a park or around your neighbourhood, absorbing the sights (along with the sounds and smells), perhaps filtering the man-made from the natural. Do you regularly honour the internal call to nature, or mindfully overcome it? Meditate while softly gazing at a beautiful flower (an African violet is one of my favourites).

---

[15] ASMR - Autonomous sensory meridian response or the tingle you get in your brain or down your spine triggered by soft sounds such as whispering, the crackling of food cooking or even gift wrapping!

Touch: e.g., textures, temperature, connection, sensual healing, massage, numbness.
Feel the objects in nature as you pass them; touch the bark of a tree; hold a stick or a conker in your hand; caress the grass, reeds or leaves; feel the heat of the Sun; stroke a pet animal.

Taste: e.g., Variety and food joy, unsafe food identification, saliva generation (to start the digestive process), required nutrient identification (in the form of a craving).
Taste your food, savour every mouthful. Allow your taste buds to come alive and sense the sweetness, sourness, bitterness, saltiness or savouriness. Be open to trying new foods and going to new places to seek them out.

Smell: e.g., pheromones, smudging, cleansing, warning of a nearby fire, spoilt food, breath, air quality, ripeness, essential oils, perfumes, aromatherapy, memory triggers.
What smells take you away instantly, often to childhood? What smells calm you? Do any energise or excite you? Do you find any supposedly normal smells nauseating? Conversely, are there some smells you like that most other people are revolted by?

Clearly, each of the five senses could be expanded upon as they are whole subjects on their own, but let's delve a little deeper with sound and then onto sight, specifically colour.

Sound

The use of sound and vibration in engineering is continually being explored and developed. From using standing waves to suspend objects in thin air to an MRI-guided ultrasound, targeted to raise the temperature of cancerous cells above fifty-five degrees and, thus, kill them. Also under development is a sonic fire extinguisher to help with the increasing problem of wildfires around the globe. A small hand-held version has been shown to put out a fire with a pulse of bass sound, generating a vibrating air column that deprives the fire of oxygen and extinguishes it. Vibrations on a larger scale, as those caused by earthquakes, can wobble or even bring down buildings at specific resonant frequencies. So, architects and engineers in seismically active zones must incorporate additional design features to improve how well a structure can withstand an earthquake. These features include using more ductile building materials, incorporating internal vibration-dampening systems and using flexible foundations and reinforced walls in the construction.

Energy, at the right frequency, can become highly potent. Perhaps certain frequencies within our vocal range are of benefit and can be used for relaxation, energising ourselves or even healing. For centuries certain tones or chants have been used to tap into such phenomena, especially in the Eastern mystical traditions.

Toning and chanting

The repetitive nature of a chant is relaxing, as cycles of breathing in and chanting out, married with the physical vibrations produced by the chant, induce a calming effect. Chanting can be combined with visualisations to bring focus on breaking up energetic blocks, supporting our immune system or attacking an illness within us.

Find a sound you are drawn to, one that resonates within you. Use it as your own form of directional ultrasound. Just as ultrasound is used to break up kidney stones, use your sound to break up emotional blockages, relax tensions or destroy diseased cells. Visualise the negative energy being diminished, eradicated and carried away by the sound into the ether. If you cannot find your own sound, try the universal chant, *Om*. Use the whole of your mouth and throat to create the chant, noticing how the sound resonates throughout your head. Play with this by varying the tone, volume and mouth position, noting any energetic shifts.

Find your sound

Find your own sound by vocally creating different noises. Play with sound using your mouth, throat and lungs. Vary everything. Change the pitch and volume, the position of the tongue or lips, and flex the throat and vocal cords. Change the breath, breathing from the belly or chest. Open and close your mouth, hum or even mouth a scream. Let out a full scream – into a pillow if you wish not to disturb anyone. Move all of your facial features as you make the sounds: screwing up your nose, pursing your lips or gyrating your jaw. Avoid using groups of words or meaningful sentences, as they are often clumsy in describing the feeling or emotion they are meant to impart. (Poets and songsmiths have wrestled with this throughout history.) Use single-syllable words, like *love, peace* or *Om* and play with their sound. Finally, find sounds that resonate with you for specific scenarios: to help with relaxation and calmness (i.e., a long nasal tone), anger (throaty), letting go (deep and guttural), joy (high pitched) and so on.

Try finding your sound as part of the *darkness* exercise from *The West* chapter.

Music

Music is not just for our listening pleasure; singers are not just entertainers. Musicians and performers indeed create music and songs we enjoy and want to sing and dance to, but they also impart something else. Music can provide a framework for healing to take place, as good a framework as provided by any shaman, priest or healer, for example. Musicians effortlessly play and wholeheartedly sing for us to feel emotion and heal if we wish to. In their own way, they drum out a beat for healing.

Music can evoke powerful emotions within us and, like many of the arts, can reflect our mood, influence our outlook and provide an outlet (and an escape) from our day-to-day lives. Film scores clearly illustrate the power of music; remove the music from a movie and its artistic appeal and emotional impact are dramatically diminished. For example, the film scores of John Williams have rightly won numerous awards, enhancing the narrative and cinematic power of scenes in the movies he has worked on, beyond anything the director and actors could solely produce. Composers, as do probably most musicians, utilise tools, techniques and sonic tricks to increase the impact of their music, creating a soundscape representing and expressing the feelings and emotions they wish to convey. When incorporated correctly, techniques such as call and response, repeated themes, harmony and dissonance, and the symbiotic relationship between major and minor keys, can take us on an emotional musical journey.

Every country and culture has traditions and wisdom to pass on, sometimes in musical form. This musical heritage, in turn, influences the younger generation and the direction of new music. The range of music is vast, but sometimes, as musicians mature, they are drawn to folk music, the music of the people. Folk music can transcend pop culture and passing fads, often containing similar messages throughout the varying folk traditions worldwide. Commonly messages of freedom, love and understanding; capturing a connection to the past with words and music.

Freedom tunes

What are your freedom tunes? Which songs or pieces of music make you want to soar? Which ones fill you with love? Conversely, what tunes make you want to weep, scream, curl up in a ball or perhaps take you to the point of despair?

Songs are powerful and take us to places, to people and back to emotionally charged events. Often there is only a short period when music is a significant factor in our lives, typically when we are young. In later life, we often listen predominately to this repertoire of songs from our youth. Hence, it is quite usual for older people to be unaware of the current music scene, and prefer the music they formed an emotional attachment to when younger. However, new songs will one day be the next generation's favourite tunes and freedom songs, so never be quick to judge how bad popular music on the radio or TV may seem to you – there is always wonderful new music, if you are open to it, but perhaps with more abrupt or cutting language. As with all music, it reflects the times and the musician's heart-felt attempt to share the emotional landscape they are exploring.

Create your freedom songs playlist, adding to it as and when you hear or remember another song that moves you. Take time choosing and putting together your playlist. Enjoy the process but also allow any emotions to come up and be released as you go through your music collection. With the advent of the internet, it is now possible to discover and download almost any song in recording history. So, if one pops into your mind that you do not own, a simple search should offer a listenable and downloadable result.

This playlist can be used to take you to various emotional places, used for ceremonial work (see below) or just put on when you are in the mood for some good music. Ensure to include upbeat songs alongside the more melancholy or sad ones so you can be taken through a whole gamut of emotions when listening.

Five songs

Choose five songs from your freedom tunes playlist that you can create a ceremony around: three songs or pieces of music that make you feel sad, one that fills you with energy and a playful or silly tune. The three sad songs should be the ones that evoke a particularly sad event or period in your life, or remind you of a departed loved one; ones that make you (or help you) cry or sob. Ones that get you every time. The song that fills you with energy can be anything that does just that. You can call this your power song. Finally, complete the playlist with a silly or playful tune, such as Monty Python's *Always look on the bright side of life*.

When you are ready to play all five songs one after the other, take an appropriate object from your altar and go into darkness. Hold onto this object and visualise the person or situation it or the songs represent, as the first three sad tunes play. Allow yourself to go deep into any emotion and release it. When the power tune is heard, move the object to the other hand and energise yourself. Feel positive, life-affirming energy filling both you and the object. You may want to move, sway or dance with this song and the energy imparted. What uplifting thoughts and positive emotions now flow around the

145

situation or person your altar object and the sad songs represent? When the final silly track is played, bring yourself back to a place of balance and lightness, allowing all the negative and positive energies to dissipate. How does your altar object feel now? Does it still represent what you thought, or has that changed? Over time, emotions around the songs may change, so keep your list updated.

Movement and shaking

Music and movement have forever been married together in dance and used throughout history as part of various spiritual practices, such as celebratory gatherings, fertility dances, dancing by a fire, entering trance-like states or acts of worship. Many customs across the globe continue these traditions, including dancing around the Maypole in the UK, the Sun Dance of the Native Americans and Middle Eastern Sufi whirling.

Using music to help you move and lose yourself is a great way to let go and enter a form of semi-trance. A tune penned by a songwriter takes you on a pre-set emotional journey. In contrast, a repetitive drumming or rattling instrumental track can aid connection with your body, shift energy and calm any mind chatter, allowing you to explore your inner world more freely.

With appropriate music, move however you see fit, but being mindful of your body. Try flowing movements, shaking, dance steps or jumping. Try going barefoot and being on the land if possible. Tune into the music and visualise as you see fit. Maybe releasing, shaking off negativity in some way, connecting to others in the present and the past, connecting to *Mother Earth* or the Universe. Give yourself permission to go wherever the music and your body take you. Move and dance with abandon.

Healing beats

Life would mean very little without beats and rhythms. From the cycle of our constant breathing or the pulse of an infectious dance beat, to the circadian rhythm of our 24 hour internal clock or the changing of the seasons, as planet Earth keeps its regular orbit around our star.

Beats and rhythms are everywhere. Starting in the womb, surrounded by fluid, the mother's heartbeat is the soundtrack to the first nine months of our lives. This rhythmic sound is so comforting and familiar that new parents use it to help their little one sleep, made evident by the number of womb sound videos available online.

Our heartbeat is a valued ally throughout our life: letting us know when we are scared or startled by wanting to jump out of our chest: pumping hard to prepare us for fight or flight: becoming a calming focus for our mind when drifting into meditation: fluttering when meeting someone we love – and seemingly stopping or breaking when we have to let them go: we hear it beating in our ears when we overexert ourselves, telling us to slow down. And then, finally, when the beat stops, our time is up. So, look after your heart as best you can. It is your connection to the rhythm of life.

Sight

Using light and immersing ourselves in various colours of the spectrum can profoundly affect our emotional state and, consequently, our well-being. The following are a few of the many colour and light exercises that can be tried.

Colour immersion

Works of art comprising blocks of colour on a large canvas (possibly only one colour), often win acclaim and elicit disdain in equal measure. Why should a six-foot square canvas painted orange be of any artistic value? Well, try standing near it and being engulfed by this colour. The colour can almost be felt when deeply looked into. One of my most profound experiences with colour was at an art installation in the UK, where a curved wall of electronic screens glowed with a block of colour, changing slowly from one to another. While standing in front of the screens, only the colour they emitted could be seen – a total immersion in this luminous energy. Afloat and adrift within it. It felt like the colour had penetrated my whole body and I was one with it; every part of my anatomy vibrating harmoniously with the colour.

Light-boxes, coloured lens glasses and virtual goggles can give a similarly immersive experience. Some cheaper alternatives are to view the world through a filter or piece of coloured plastic, gaze at coloured paper or download coloured screen savers or similar for your laptop, tablet or phone. Gazing softly at a sunset or lying on the ground and looking up at the blue sky are also great ways to lose yourself in colour.

According to Eastern tradition, the major organs are directly linked to our internal energy centres, known as chakras, and the use of colour is one of the ways to help bring them into balance.

Try visualising a cloud of each colour swirling around and through your body, bathing and saturating it in healing energy. Allow the colours to move and merge as you work with them – as we are not simply a heart and mind but a digestive tract, nervous system, glands, bones, muscles, etc., all functioning together.

The descriptions below are a guide only, so please use your intuition, as we all react differently to each colour.

Red: An energising colour, known to loosen, open and release stiffness and constrictions. Beneficial for anaemia and blood-related conditions.

Orange: Has a freeing action upon the mind and body. Orange is a warm colour, the colour of the setting sun. It can help to bring about new ideas and can help deal with surplus sexual expression.

Yellow: Associated with strengthening the nerves and mind. A good colour for those who suffer from a nervous disposition.

Green: Universal healing colour. Good for blood pressure and issues of the heart. It has both an energising and soothing effect.

Blue : A soothing colour used for ailments and constrictions associated with speech and communication.

Indigo: It is known to purify the mind. Good for dealing with ailments within the eyes and ears, and stabilising mental problems.

Violet: Colour of spirit, not generally used for physical conditions. Good for opening and expanding psychic pathways.

White: White light is comprised of all the colours so it is often associated with perfection and God/Goddess. It can be used for direct connection to the Divine, general self-healing and replacing released negative energies.

Silver/Gold: Shimmering and reflective, these colours are good for energising the body and mind or reflecting away negative energies. Useful in attracting wealth and abundance.

Converse with the body

The cells in our body are constantly in flux, being replaced whenever they come to the end of their effective life. The rate of change varies depending on the cell type. For example, stomach and intestinal cells are replaced every five or so days, skin cells every two to four weeks and liver cells every five months. Cells in the skeletal system regenerate almost constantly, but the complete process takes a full ten years, with this renewal process slowing down as we age[16].

If cells are being created continuously, the more we can be in a pleasant and comfortable state, the higher the chance the cells will be created healthily. Conversely, if we are in a constant state of stress or agitation, the cells created are open to taking on this negative energy. Does it seem possible that particularly vulnerable cells could mutate into cancerous ones during a period of prolonged stress? There is no concrete proof of this from trials conducted by the UK National Health Service, but like many esoteric ideas, I suggest using your discernment.

When in meditation, talk to your body, focussing on each area as you do so. Create a dialogue between you and your individual parts.

[16] Chris Opfer, *Does your body really replace itself every seven years?*, Updated Apr 2021, *Howsstuffworks.com.*

Pose questions and wait for answers. For example, ask, "How are you, heart?", "Can I do anything for you, lungs?" or "Liver, what should I do to help you today?" Try asking the varying parts of your body what colour you need to work with to help clear blockages and keep each area healthy, being mindful that this may change each time you do the exercise.

Visualise the colour floating in a ball in front of your face. Gently inhale this colourful energy and allow it to move to where it is needed, bathing and soothing the organ or area. With the exhale, see the same colour blown out, but now carrying away any blockage or energetic impurities. Repeat this cycle of inhaling and exhaling, keeping the energetic colour flowing. If drawn to, combine this practice with the work on illness and disease described in *The South* section.

Running the rainbow

Running the rainbow is a lovely exercise connecting to the beauty and colour of a rainbow and linking to the four classical elements. A rainbow is the product of the Sun's energy in the form of light (*fire*), refracted in the atmosphere (*air*) through raindrops (*water*) that have formed around dust particles (*earth*). It is one of the most beautiful sights in nature and can be used spiritually as the gift it is. The rainbow is an arc of light, as seen from our perspective (it is actually a circle if viewed from above), with a beginning and end. But, as we know, the end of the rainbow cannot be reached – nor can that elusive pot of gold! This is true, but when working energetically with rainbows, we can change the rules.

Find stillness, either sitting or lying down, and visualise a rainbow, with you sitting at one end of it. Bring each colour down in turn, filling yourself with each. Surround yourself with an aura of each colour. A *Ready Brek*[17] glow of red, orange, yellow, green, sky blue, indigo and violet.

How does each colour feel? Are any colours out of balance? If one feels weaker than the other, expand it – make it stronger, more vibrant, more energetic. Maybe a reason for the imbalance will be shown to you. Now allow the full spectrum of colours to flow into your body, filling you with a myriad of colour; rainbows swirling within you. Allow the colours to move, blend and pulse throughout your physical and energetic body, finding balance.

Finally, come to a sitting position with hands on your thighs or knees, palms facing up, and visualise a rainbow coming out of one palm, arcing over and going into the other. Vary the width of your hands and allow the rainbow to change size appropriately. Allow the rainbow to move from your hands and enter your body. Again feel the energy, beauty and healing power. Fill every space with a spectrum of colour.

Play with these techniques. Vary the size of the rainbow or the colour intensities. Visualise clouds, wind and rain, as rain is always required for a rainbow. Feel your chaotic storm energies subside and dissipate as the rainbow appears, as the colours soothe you. A rainbow can then have a more profound meaning the next time you see one.

---

[17] *Ready Brek* is a breakfast cereal that has had UK advertising campaigns, starting in the 1970s, showing the children who ate it surrounded by a warm orange glow.

Using spells and potions
Note: Safety warning

To my mind, spells are reinforced prayers; asking for help ceremonially by combining the prayer with an everyday object such as a candle or wooden stick. The spell can be scratched into a candle before lighting or carved on a stick before being burnt. Alternatively, a spell can be written on a piece of paper that can be burnt ceremonially. The mixing of herbs, plants or other natural items for potions and spells is a sizeable subject on its own and not covered in any detail here. Medicines come from the natural world, so I suggest concocting potions for spells and healing is founded on strong roots (literally).

You can create your own potions without any knowledge of herbalism by using medically non-active ingredients and ceremonially mixing them. Use a decorative pot or jar and bless any water or liquid used. With an intention in mind, imbibe the mixture with positive energy and loving thoughts by adding pleasant-smelling liquids, flower petals, leaves, sweets or cake decorations and anything you feel would add to the mixture's potency. In the Q'ero tradition I have been taught, this potion is known as a *limpia* (*clean* in Spanish). It is a potion filled with love and, as the name suggests, used to help clean the soul. A *limpia* can be used to bless the earth and sacred objects or anoint yourself and others. However, please do not drink it. The Q'ero use a different method to create potions taken internally, but I am not covering that in this book.

Always make any potion or spell positive, as you would a prayer. Never make it negative with the intent of harming another. As with any spiritual work, if you ask for something negative to happen to someone, be prepared for it to come back to you – and not in a good way. The purpose of using spiritual energy, prayers, spells, potions or similar is to help weave a wonderful life for you, your family, your community, the more-than-human world and, ultimately, all life on this planet.

Creation

Creation is the most potent force in the Universe. From the Big Bang to conception. It drives expansion. It is the essence of the Universe. Being creative, in whatever way you choose, benefits your mental, physical and spiritual wellbeing. Anything artistic, whatever you can lose yourself in or makes your world a little more beautiful, is an excellent use of time.

There are various ways to be creative, not only as an artistic expression but in all you do. Perhaps look at areas where you may feel a little stale or stuck. Try new methods or techniques, incorporate new ideas, review how others do something similar (online videos are great for this) and see if anything resonates with you.

Create your symbol

Symbols can bypass the consciousness and enter the subconsciousness. Hence the power of corporate logos and marketing.

Write a sentence describing what you want your symbol to stand for. Maybe it is a desire, a dream, or to represent yourself. Write down this desire or, if it is to represent you, write your full name. Then remove the vowels and any repeated letters, reducing the words to a few key letters. Rearrange these letters into a symbol that resonates with your intention. If nothing is forthcoming, play with lines and move the shapes around until you find a symbol you are happy with. Write this symbol out several times and become familiar with it. Then be creative with it. Paint or draw your symbol, carve it into wood, create jewellery using it or put it on a t-shirt. Use your symbol in ceremony. It is your symbol. Fill it with power.

Share the love exercise

Sit in front of a mirror and look at yourself. Let love radiate from your eyes, into the eyes of your reflection and back again, bouncing between the two. Feel a warm, fuzzy, peaceful love expand from your heart and out through your eyes. Let any negative thoughts go and focus on generating love. How easy is this for you to do? Are there any blocks? Do you feel silly? Are you hung up on how you look? Can you see beyond the physical? Work on this until you can. When you feel connected to the love in your heart and the love you are radiating, take a moment to accept the love for yourself. You are worthy to both give and receive this potent love.

Let the love, and the feeling of love, encompass your whole body. Then allow it to overflow and spread, filling first the room you are in, then going further, throughout the building, into the street, the town and beyond. Feel it radiate to those around you, your friends and family, the community, the country and the whole planet. Bathe everything in love. Imagine a wave of loving heart threads emanating from you, carrying this love far and wide. Visualise and feel it being received by all you are sending it to, by the people, the plants and animals, by *Mother Earth* and *Father Sky*. Sense the gratitude come back, in return for this gift of love you have freely given.

While still in this bubble of radiating love, bring your focus back to yourself and send love to any areas of your body you think may need it; any part of your psyche you wish to 'love on'. Send healing, loving energy to any worries or troublesome situations, people and animals suffering or any worldwide concerns. Send love to wherever you feel it is needed. Take a moment to connect with the ancestors and share the love with them, feeling their love in return. Connect to your parents, grandparents, great-grandparents and the countless generations. Finally, if you are drawn to it, send love to any spirit guides, gurus or deities as a thank-you for their help and guidance.

This exercise can be done with another person or in pairs within a group situation. Sit facing each other at arm's length and look into each other's eyes. Repeat the word "love" in your mind and show this love through your eyes. Don't look for love in the other person's eyes; only radiate love from yours. Continue to look, even if you feel uncomfortable. Keep going beyond any inhibitions. This sharing of love is open and honest with no strings attached. No promises are being made. Only a pure exchange of love energy. Love is an abundant energy, so you can keep giving it without ever losing it. In fact, the more you give, the more your receive. So sharing your love is not being wasteful, and there is no need to receive any in return, as you can always generate more love energy yourself. However, the other person will likely respond in kind and share their love, growing the love energy between you.

All manner of emotions may come up for one or both of you. Smiles, laughter, playfulness, desires, sadness, painful memories or heartbreak. Play with it, but try to spend at least ten minutes in this space, finishing in a positive place. When completed, embrace if you wish and spend a moment in gratitude for what each has shared. No words other than thank you are needed. Don't feel pressured into saying any more once the exercise is over unless you wish to. This is not a romantic or sexual exercise, so it does not matter if the other person is your partner or not.

It is very empowering, albeit a little unsettling, to do this exercise with a stranger in a group setting, but well worth getting over any inhibitions to give it a go.

Ancestral honouring

"You're just like your father" or "I sound just like my mother", are commonly spoken phrases throughout households in the UK. We inherit so much, not only physical characteristics but our mannerisms, behaviours and beliefs. No upbringing is perfect and it is up to the individual to recognise and make changes if needed. This is easier said than done, as inherited patterns become ingrained, behaviours change into habits and genes (currently) are ours for life. List the traits of your parents, both good and bad. Which are in you?

Create a ceremony of thanks for the gifts they have given you. Be thankful for giving you life and all the love and teachings, care and support, safety and security they provided. Also, acknowledge the not-so-good things that you are now ready to forgive and release, be it their anger, pain, quick temper, apologetic attitude, lack of self-esteem, constant judging, overbearing nature, etc. Use one or more of the exercises from *The South* to let go of anything negative. Having an object on your altar representing one or both of your parents is usually beneficial, as there is often much to work upon in this area. If you feel that you had a relatively good upbringing, it is still worth having a mother and father object as it strengthens your connection to them and honours the love they have (or had) for you and your love for them.

Female lineage connection

Use the mother object from your altar, or an object that represents female energy to you, and conduct this exercise with a focus on the your family's female lineage.

While holding the object, visualise your mother standing behind you, her hands on your shoulders. It doesn't matter if she is alive or in spirit. Imagine she is with you today for this ceremony. Continue visualising your female lineage standing behind her, ancestral mothers with hands on their daughter's shoulders going back as far as you can imagine. Even if you did not know your mother, grandmother or great-grandmother, visualise women standing in a line, one behind the other. Link into this lineage. What is being passed down? What do the mothers wish for their daughters? What teaching and wisdom is being shared? Then, if you have a daughter, imagine her standing in front of you, your hands on her shoulders. What are you passing on? What have you not passed on? Why not? Where are the blocks? Do this for each of your daughters and continue with any granddaughters or great-granddaughters. If you do not have a daughter, imagine you do and visualise putting your hands on her shoulders. How does that feel? Do you want to raise a daughter? What would your hopes and dreams be for her?

When you are ready, visualise yourself turning and facing your mother, taking her hands in yours. Can you look her in the eyes? What comes up? Do either of you want to say anything to each other? Finally, thank her. Thank her for the gift of life, for carrying you in her womb, and for all she has given and provided you. Continue with this gratitude, extending it to your whole lineage, thanking the women that came before and the women to come after you. If you haven't already, include the mothers from your father's side too.

Male lineage connection

Similarly to the *female lineage* exercise, hold the father object from your altar and visualise your father standing behind you, his hands on your shoulders. Imagine he is with you today for this ceremony, whether he is alive or in spirit. Visualise his father standing behind him with his hands on your father's shoulders. Continue with your male lineage, your ancestral fathers with hands on their son's shoulders, going back as far as you can imagine. Don't worry about accurately seeing their faces; just allow the images to come. If there are no images, simply sense this long male line. Link into this lineage. What is being passed down? What does each father wish for his son? What teachings or wisdom are being shared? How does this feel?

Then, if you have a son, imagine him standing in front of you, your hands on his shoulders. What are you passing on? What energy is there between you? What have you not shared? Why not? Do the same for each of your sons and continue with any grandsons or great-grandsons. If you do not have a son, imagine you do and put your hands on his shoulders. How does that feel? Do you want to raise a son? What would your hopes and dreams be for him?

When you are ready, visualise yourself turning and facing your father, putting your hands on his shoulders and him doing the same, or holding onto each others arms if you cannot reach. Can you look him in the eyes? What comes up? Do either of you want to say anything to each other? Thank him. Thank him for the gift of life and all he has given and provided you. Continue with this gratitude and extend it to your entire male lineage, thanking the men that came before and the men to come after you. If you haven't already, include the fathers on your mother's side of the family.

Note: Ceremonies have been known to have taken place at least 35,000 years ago, so let's take this figure as a baseline for homo sapiens that show similarities to us emotionally and intellectually. [In fact, our brain has been the same size for 300,000 years and the same shape for 30,000 - 100,000 years[18], so this figure is probably conservative.] Based on an average age of eighteen for a woman to give birth, the figure of 35,000 years gives the number of previous generations as approximately two thousand. Therefore, to visualise your sentient ancestors would require a line of almost two thousand people, stretching back for well over a kilometre or close to one mile. Two thousand generations as capable and undoubtedly as curious and intelligent, in their own way, as modern man and woman. What was learnt by these generations that has been lost? What was learnt by those far more connected and in tune with the land? Over the millennia, what evolution has taken place? What changes have human beings undergone over two thousand generations? These are some interesting questions to ponder.

As another note, some Buddhist monks create intricate mandalas from different coloured sand as part of their spiritual practice, often to honour those that have gone before - as they believe we are made from grains of our ancestors.

Additional exercises:

1) Connect with both parents and all of your ancestors
Before you close the space, you may wish to expand the above visualisations to embrace both parents, imagining them with one hand on each of your shoulders. Then their parents before them and so on, fanning back through your entire ancestry. Feel your lineage flow into you. Let the energy build inside you. What are the teachings? Is there balance between male and female?

---

[18] Neubauer, Hublin and Gunz, *The evolution of modern human brain shape*, published in *Science Advances*, 24 Jan 2018.

You currently stand at the forefront of millions of years of evolution. It has taken 13.7 billion years, the age of the known Universe, to reach this point. All that history, all that evolutionary adaptation, has culminated in you. You have every right to be here and are very special indeed.

Note: If there is an adoption in your family history, include this additional branch of your tree. Both your biological and non-biological parents played a role. Bear in mind that if you go back two thousand generations, it is quite probable you will have an adoption somewhere in your lineage. You are also likely to be linked to the whole gamut of humanity from nobility to pauper, priest to thief, builder to philosopher, healer to life taker.

2) Cutting the ancestral ties
While carrying out the ancestral connection work outlined above, you may wish to transmute any negative energies or inherited traits that no longer serve. A simple way to cut these ancestral ties is by energetically cutting the negative threads woven through your lineage, possibly even passed onto your offspring.

To cut the ties, imagine a cord of negative energy coming into you from your ancestors, passing through and out of you. Cut this chord off, both entering and leaving, using a visualised sword, knife, energy beam or similar. See it disintegrate and shatter off into sparkles of light, dispersing into the ether. Pull out any strands from your body and blow them away as dust in the air. Feel the negative connection being severed and dissolving into the ether. If you feel more work is to be done in this area, try using one of the previous *letting go* exercises from *The South* section, but with the focus on your ancestral lineage.

Inner child work

Get to know your inner child; from the time you were a baby through infancy to childhood. *Little you*. What are your earliest memories? Try to fill in the rest of the time from when you were conceived to your first memories. Where were you born? What was your house and local area like? Do you have photos? Have you spoken to your parents about your birth and infancy? If they are not around to talk to, is there another family member you can ask? Revisit the places of your childhood: old haunts, schools, parks, friends or aunts/uncles/grandparents' houses that you frequented, places where incidents you remember occurred. Where do your childhood memories want to lead you back to? Write about these places if it is not practical to visit. What emotions come up? Release any negativity. Rekindle the joys and positives of your childhood.

Write a letter to your inner child. Start it with "Dear Little [insert your name]". What do you want to say to your younger self, age four or five, *Little you*? What advice and teachings do you want to share? What warnings, if any? Is there any regret over failed plans or broken promises? What apologies do you want to make? Is there any sorrow or guilt? Be as honest and open as possible, allowing emotion to flow. If tears come, let them. Let them fall onto the paper you write on, adding another level of emotional intensity to this deeply personal process. When finished, put the letter in an envelope and address it, "To Little [insert your name]".

Then write a letter from your inner child to you, but this time write using your non-normal hand. This will take concentration, allowing you to focus on the words and the emotions that arise, and probably make the writing look like a child's. Start the letter with "Dear Big [insert your name]." What does *Little you* want to say to *Big you*? What were your dreams, aspirations and hopes for the future? How did *Little you* feel? Did they feel safe when young or, at times, vulnerable? What emotions were going on? Was there fear? Was there love? What was *Little you's* relationship with your parents like? Take yourself back to your younger self, even if only in spirit, if the memories are too distant. Embody this inner child energy and write from the heart. When finished, put this letter into an envelope marked, "To Big [insert your name]".

You now have two letters, one from you to your inner child and another from your inner child to you. Keep these letters for a period, to review and contemplate upon. Are there any commonalities, any themes running through both? What areas can you work on? When you feel ready, let go of the letters by burning them ceremonially or posting them to the Universe, ensuring they cannot find their way back to you.

Childhood photo board and video story

Collate photographs of yourself, from a baby to adulthood, creating a collage on a large piece of card, cork board or similar. A digital collage is fine, but print out a decent hard copy that can be pinned up. Let the photos tell the story of you growing physically. Use the most powerful pictures, good or bad. What emotion does this bring up? Are there any photos that exhibit a different emotion from what you thought you had at the time? Maybe during a difficult period, you felt you were constantly miserable, but the photos clearly show you were happy. How do the emotions you pick up from the photos fit with your physical appearance at the time? Were you comfortable with how you looked?

If your life has been documented via video camera or smartphone, try editing a video montage of your birth and adolescence, again collating the good and bad, and noticing what emotions are triggered. Update your *Life CV* with any forgotten childhood events.

Childlike vs childish and asking for help

Being childish means behaving like a child and reacting as a child would, with such behaviour in an adult linked to a lack of emotional intelligence if displayed regularly. Even so, this behaviour can often be witnessed in successful and prominent people across the globe, from world leaders and heads of corporations to sports people and celebrities. A tantrum is still a tantrum, at whatever age it is stamped out. Being childlike is different. It is in that space of innocence, wonder and awe, a place of trust and exploration, where discovery and adventure come naturally, as it does to children.

Firstly, to overcome the societal and cultural pressures of having to behave like an adult, give yourself permission to be a child once more. Allow yourself the time and space to explore what it means to be a child again. Connect to your inner child. If you have written the letters to and from your inner child, the connection should be clearer and easier to make.

A childlike state naturally opens us up to the signs of the Universe, the messages and energies that come to us daily. In this state, we absorb information and experiences, just as children do. So try babbling like a toddler, crawling around like an infant (noticing the new perspective), playing with a stick or gazing at a flower. Watch the ants, marvel at a spider's web, lose yourself in a painting or dive into a photo. Dress up as a cowboy, a princess, an astronaut. Play football and pretend to score the winning goal in the World Cup.

Visualise yourself on stage winning the final of a talent show. Splash in a puddle or skip through the woods, kicking up autumnal leaves. Play with life a little. We were all children once and still are children at heart, so remember how to play.

Children have no problem asking for help, as they instinctively want to learn. Asking for help reinforces that we do not know everything; it shows humility. As we all are children spiritually, why not ask for help from your subconscious, spiritual guides or the Divine? Wouldn't it, or they want to help? As conscious beings with free will, it is up to us to ask for help and, just as importantly, to wait for and be open to the reply.

Simple methods of asking for help are prayer, meditation, shamanic journeying, letter writing, conversing with nature or even pilgrimage to a significant place. Praying and asking God for help is fine if you believe in God. If you doubt or do not believe, you need a comparable method of call and response – asking for help and listening for the answer. This can be found with meditation, journeying and communing with the natural world. A pilgrimage doesn't necessarily have to be to a religious site; it can just as easily be to a place in nature you are drawn to. Following in the footsteps of others who have held the quest for help in their heart can bolster your determination to find answers for yourself.

We learn best from teachers because, as children, we instinctively believed what authority figures told us. They were trusted and we accepted that grown-ups were trying to help us. Sadly, that trust can be broken. If you have ever experienced such a betrayal, I strongly suggest working on this to clear as much of the emotional charge, negative thought patterns and unconscious energy around it. The exercises around letting go, forgiveness and inner child work will assist with this.

Therefore, when asking for help with an issue, put yourself into a childlike state and play with the process. Remember to listen for the answer and not be surprised if it seems comical, fantastical or simplistic to you as an adult. It is being presented in a way that your inner child would understand.

Being childlike, as opposed to childish, can have its rewards. Never lose contact with that inner child and a youthful outlook on life. It keeps the journey fresh and joyful, and acts as a beacon to those that cross your path.

Those that have gone before

We have always shared and passed on our thoughts and ideas, philosophies and opinions, our stories and advice. For most of human history this was only by oral tradition, but since the advent of language, the written word has dominated; initially on clay and stone, then on papyrus scrolls and, since the invention of the printing press, in newspapers and books. Most recently, our words have been stored and shared digitally or even recorded as audio and video media, adding emotion and colour to what we want to say. What cannot be recorded are our feelings. Only the words, music or visual representations attempting to describe our feelings. By taking action – by experiencing and discovering things for ourselves – we can explore and, to some degree, replicate these feelings, understanding why certain spiritual practices have been passed down through the generations. Through replication and practice, we find our connection to the past strengthened.

There are those that have gone before, who have sat where you have sat, looked out from where you have looked out, thought about what you have thought about. As new as every day may seem to us, as unique as we believe we are as individuals, many others have felt similarly to us. So, try gazing in wonder at a sunset or the moon and connect to the millions who have done so before you. Or swim under a waterfall and feel the magical presence of those who have swum or possibly even been blessed in that place over the years.

It is, in some part, from the activities of those that have gone before – their energetic echo – that places become sacred, buildings holy. This energy builds in these sites, particularly in beautiful natural locations. This is akin to what Rupert Sheldrake coined as *morphic resonance*[19] – an inherited memory passed down through the generations that builds up the spiritual energy of a place. Take a moment in such places to feel the connection to the past, to those that have gone before, allowing gratitude to flow.

Ancestors around the fire

People have sat around fire for as long as there have been people. Fire has provided light, warmth, security and a means of cooking food. It is a place of gathering and sharing. A place of ceremony and celebration. A place of storytelling and imagination. Fire has been gazed upon in wonderment and enraptured many a captivated mind for generations. One could even label fire nature's TV, to give it a modern spin.

Light a candle or, if you have access to one, light a real fire and sit in front of that. Get comfortable and let your gaze dwell on the candle flame or fire before gently softening your focus or closing your eyes. Sense, feel or imagine yourself in nature, sitting in a clearing next to an open fire. In your visualisation gaze softly into the fire, feeling its warmth. Sense the connection to all the fires

---

[19] Rupert Sheldrake, Morphic Resonance: The Nature of Formative Causation, 2009, Park Street Press.

around the globe and to all the fires there have ever been, along with the many people who have sat around them.

Begin by giving thanks to those that have come before you, those that have walked the earth where you are now and, at some point in history, sat around an open fire where (or very near to where) you are physically doing this visualisation. The UK, for example, has been inhabited for at least thirteen thousand years, and I suggest fires have been lit within eyeshot of almost every square metre of land during that time.

Continue by inviting your family and ancestors, alive or in spirit, to share the fire with you. Imagine them sitting in rings around you and the fire, the first ring comprised of your immediate family, the second their parents and so on outwards. Visualise circles of ancestors present with you in this liminal place, coming to share the fire. There may be non-humans wanting to be there with you too: animals, deities, ascended masters, etc. Anyone or anything can turn up. Go back as far as you like and be swamped in the largest fire circle ever known, with you sitting next to the fire in the centre. Feel surrounded by your supporting crowd, cheering you on. All who have come are there because of you. All are there for you. How does that make you feel? Put yourself in your ancestors' shoes and look down upon the gathering. Is there wisdom to be imparted? Are there any messages for you?

Be with this imagery, knowing that you have every right to be sitting where you are, representing all who have gone before. Feel the love, feel the energy and allow yourself to be humbled by the privilege you have been given. You may wish to dance, sing, chant, drum or rattle in this fire circle, in your mind or even wherever you are physically. Do so. Do whatever you feel helps honour your ancestors around this fire. Play with this. If something feels disrespectful or

incorrect, stop, apologise to those present and try something else. Mistakes, as has been said before, are a part of learning and growth.

When you feel you have finished, give a final thanks to those that have come to your fire, bring yourself out of the visualisation and spend a reflective moment gazing at your candle or open fire. To take this further, try conducting your own fire ceremony (see the *Mother Earth* section.)

Grandmother and grandfather energy

The terms grandmother or grandfather energy refer to the energy that emanates from a long-lived person. A wise elder. Someone who has lived a full life, learnt from their mistakes, successfully raised children, helped the family and community, is full of wisdom (but still open to learning), has nothing to prove, has no need to compete, realises that everyone has a right to their own spirituality, is connected to their environment, laughs a lot, is generous, has a kind *lived-in* face, is happy, content and at peace with themselves.

Sound wonderful, don't they? Can you tap into this energy? Do (or did) either of your grandparents exhibit such characteristics? If they did, incorporate your grandmother and grandfather in your meditation; otherwise, invite imagined, wonderful and benevolent grandmothers or grandfathers to come and be with you. Use the *Ancestors around the fire* visualisation or the stone circle journey from the *Contemporary shamanism* section as a basis for a connecting meditation or visualisation. Converse with the grandmothers and grandfathers. Feel worthy of absorbing any wisdom. Allow it to embrace and engulf you. Give thanks for such a powerful birthright.

Ancestor box

If you have objects, trinkets or keepsakes from loved ones, try collecting them together in a suitable box or container. This can then become your ancestor box. Keeping these items in one place can aid ancestral honouring and help with the realisation that what has come down through your lineage, the gift of your life today, is only because of every single one of your ancestors – the whole of your lineage since the dawn of time. If there were a break in the chain, you would not be here. You may want to keep this box on or near your altar. What stories do the items tell? Can any items be passed on or given away? If not, why not? What advice would the ancestors the objects represent want to give you?

The East - **The bigger picture, vision and dreams**

*"One doesn't discover new lands without consenting to
lose sight of the shore for a very long time."*
Andre Gide.

The East is represented by Eagle or Condor. It is about looking at
things from a different perspective and seeing the bigger picture.
Condor's sharp eyesight invites us to focus on our dreams, even if
they seem far away, and shows us that we can see further when we
fly high and gain a broad overview. Just as Condor soars effortlessly
high above, in a world we can only gaze at from the ground, *The
East* is the direction where we begin to explore our connection to all
that is beyond and to what is outside of us, more specifically to the
Great Mystery and the Divine.

Do you know what you want? What are your dreams, your desires,
your life goals? What steps have you made towards them? Does
anything need to change? A Condor's viewpoint is forever moving
as she soars across the skies. The ground below, however, is more
static in nature. But, even here, erosion, fire, animal activity, human
development, etc., changes the landscape over time. Nothing is
static. Change is everywhere. We too can, and do, change.

What is your medicine?

In this case, when referring to medicine, I am not talking about a
prescribed pill or tonic but the characteristics and traits you possess
that help yourself, your community and the world around you. What
are you good at? What are your gifts? What is your arena? What

were your parent's gifts? Have you inherited any? Were you born to play an instrument, sing, create art, grow things, organise, be a healer, make people laugh, be an accountant, footballer, engineer, carer, mother or father? Where does your passion lie? What you love, what you are drawn to, what you are good at, can be termed *your medicine.*

Singers have to sing, musicians have to play, dancers have to dance, comedians have to entertain people, sportsmen and women have to compete. It is clear, most obviously within the arts and sports, that some people were born to do what they do. Jimi Hendrix to play the guitar, Karen Carpenter to sing, Keith Moon to play the drums, George Best to play football, Robert De Niro to act, Mo Farah to run, Pablo Picasso to paint and Shakespeare to write. These people, along with many others with a passion for what they do, feel something more. A compulsion to do it, a necessity. They have to follow this calling, or else they are depriving themselves of some part (perhaps a large part) of life as they see it. Playing the instrument, competing in their sport, singing their songs, immersing themselves in the character or creating the artwork is *in their blood*; a significant component of who they are and often when they feel most comfortable and confident expressing themselves.

We all have this to some extent, perhaps not as obvious or prevalent as those mentioned above or others we can think of, but it is still there nonetheless. Our own medicine. So what is yours? Immersed in what action does your heart beat fastest? What would you do if you could do anything? What do you have to do?

Maybe some of the most potent examples of people embodying their medicine had something special, something different from us mere mortals. Let us call it a genius gene. This genius gene, or X factor, helped drive them to express their talent as far as possible. To break new ground, create something unique or achieve new heights, raising the bar in their field. It is a driver of evolution. Pushing the limits, so that the next generation can push them further still. However, having this gene, or more accurately, this desire, should not be a goal in and of itself; some people have been consumed by this aspirational behaviour, becoming obsessive, delusional or deeply depressed at never achieving the unattainable goals they set themselves. 'Live fast, die young' is not a motto of the enlightened soul. So living your dreams and following your heart, as good advice as it is, must be tempered with a healthy outlook and consideration for your body and mind. Follow your passion, but not at the expense of your health.

Once you have identified your medicine, look to embrace it within your life as best you can. How can it be manifested within your vocation, your home, your family or within the community? Find ways to share it as much as possible so that its benefit can be felt by many. Work with your medicine, not against it. Often though, to work with your medicine, to give it the focus it deserves, means removing some of the clutter from your mind and life. Making space for the new. Hopefully, some of the exercises from *The South, The West* and *The North* have helped with this clearing and healing process, opening the way to go deeper by flying higher, as Condor teaches.

What is normal?

It is deemed culturally acceptable to want to fit in, to belong. We are regularly told that we are social animals and it is beneficial to our health to be around others, to interact and have relationships. This was highlighted during the coronavirus pandemic when social interactions were curtailed and feelings of isolation were widespread. We like to be in our comfort zone by being around those who look, sound and dress similarly to us and perhaps even hold similar views. Many people want to belong – to be part of something bigger than themselves – and be part of a tribe of sorts. This may shed some light on the pleasure of supporting a particular sporting team, trends in fashion, or even getting a particular tattoo. Conversely, and more seriously, when people are deemed not to fit in, individuals or whole groups can be open to trolling, verbal abuse, persecution, physical violence or even the threat of death from their tormentors. This bigotry and persecution are likely to result in, at the very least, mental trauma, but also physical health issues, suicidal thoughts or fleeing for one's life to another place or country and seeking asylum.

We are, of course, all human and, in that sense, similar, but we also know that we are unique and are probably glad we are, even if, at times, we may feel that we don't fit in. However, being different is an essential part of being normal: that is, normal from a statistical point of view.

The figure below illustrates how a group of people (or population) can be measured against any characteristic or category. The characteristic is along the bottom or X axis, and the quantity or number of occurrences is on the vertical or Y axis. Generally, most populations produce a bell-shaped curve when measured against most characteristics. This indicates that most of the population is towards the middle – nearer the average – with fewer occurrences at the extremes of the characteristic.

For example, if the category on the bottom axis was male height, most men would be between 5'3" and 6'4" (1.6m-1.93m). The number would reduce as the sizes became smaller and taller, down to one person at either end of the spread. In 2014, according to Wikipedia, the world's shortest man was Chandra Bahadur Dangi, from Nepal, at 0.55m (21.5 inches), and the world's tallest man was

Sultan Kosen, from Turkey, at 2.67m (8 foot 9 inches). All other men would be in between when comparing their height.

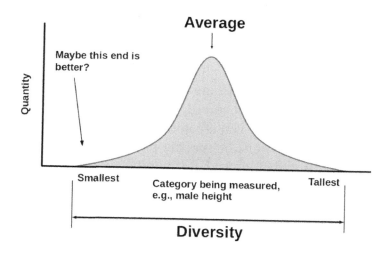

The people towards the extremes of this curve, the shortest and tallest, have undoubtedly had various comments throughout their lives about their size. Sadly these comments may be negative and spiteful, reinforcing to the receiver that they are not normal. In fact, this is not statistically true, as the whole of the population under the line is *normal*. This is what a normal population looks like. It has two thinner tails and a large middle hump. The hump is where the average lies, where the mean, median and mode averages sit. Being on the edge, in the tails, is still normal, simply further away from the average. Further away from the middle can be thought of as sometimes positive and sometimes negative, just as being average can have a dual meaning.

In this height example, maybe it is better to be towards the left tail in some instances. If one is smaller than average, there are advantages to be had with regards leg room on planes, a likely lower spend on food and never having to worry about bumping into low doorways or ceilings. Both extremes have advantages and disadvantages, and yes, they are different from the average, but still very much normal. The spread shows a population's diversity, with the whole group in question fitting under the curve and, most importantly, statistically normal.

So, even if you feel you are one of a kind, you are still normal because you fit the statistical spread. Someone has to be at the limit. Why not you? Yes, maybe you are not average in certain areas, such as particular character traits or specific physical measurements, but that is life. That is variation. And, it is normal.

Who are you? The roles we play in life

If you were asked the question, "Who are you?", how would you respond? Your name? Your sex? Your nationality? How about your job or marital status? Are these the things that define you? Look around your home. What represents you? What do your home, the objects you own, the area where you live, your nationality and culture say about who you think you are?

List out answers to the question, "Who am I?" Here are a few to get you going. A woman, a plumber, a housekeeper, a friend, a carer, an animal, a collection of atoms, a student, a teacher, a sister, a machine, a dreamer, an organiser, a father. Be creative and see how many you can come up with.

This list is likely to be much longer than you initially thought. It shows that you have and play out, many roles in life. In fact, we are much more than we think we are and therefore are likely to have more gifts and skills than perhaps we thought we did.

As human beings, we are incredible creatures. Amazing machines that convert food to fuel, continually grow and replace cells, heal ourselves from injuries and illnesses, adapt to many environments and conditions, are waterproof but can breathe, are heat resistant but can sweat to sustain an optimal operating temperature, and have an internal pump that can function 24/7 for upwards of a hundred years! Then we have our brain. That collection of billions of neurons that spark with electricity allowing us to learn, dream, analyse, discern, remember, calculate, be aware and, arguably, where our consciousness resides.

But for all our amazing physiology, biology and chemistry, we can easily be enslaved and indoctrinated, be moulded or influenced by our upbringing, surroundings and thoughts. As Henry Ford said, "Whether you think you can, or you think you can't – you're right."

Are your core beliefs yours? How many are inherited or imposed upon you by circumstance? Looking through the roles you have played or are playing, which ones are who you want to be? Can you let go of the ones holding you back, the ones that no longer serve you? Try ceremonially letting go of these unwanted roles by writing them on individual pieces of paper or small sticks and burning them.

What roles do you want to keep – the ones you love and truly feel like you? What new roles would you like to explore, learn or embody? Create another list of aspirational new roles, linked maybe to your vision board (see later) and write an affirmation (also see later) around them. Try being creative with these roles. Create an artwork to reflect them or write a song or a piece of music that encapsulates them. Begin to dream your world into being.

You may feel some anger when carrying out the above exercises as you realise that elements of who you thought you were, are not the real you, or, at least, not the person you now wish to be. This is OK and understandable, as you have to accept that the usual way of raising children is common and goes largely unchallenged. As creatures of habit, we bring up children (if we have them) similarly to how we were raised, possibly changing a few things we remember not liking from our childhood but, by and large, fitting into the cultural and societal norms. So, forgive your parents; they were undoubtedly trying their best. Forgive the community and culture within which you were raised, as this has been moulded over many years by people also trying their best and, perhaps, knew no better way.

Sadly, it seems that in today's westernised societies, no government has the vision or ability to create a utopian world, a world perhaps portrayed in fantasy or science fiction, where humanity has moved beyond power struggles, money, ownership, overconsumption, inequalities, colour or creed. This utopia is currently only found in small pockets around the globe, in enlightened families and communities. That said, the ideals they live by can be embraced by anyone and, in my opinion, are within every human heart, albeit sometimes buried, hidden or tarnished with indoctrination and untruths.

Only each of us as individuals can create the joy of life: imagined as thoughts, expressed in our behaviours and finally realised by our actions. It is unlikely that any mainstream organisation, company or government has the vision or altruistic incentive to do this for us. It is a bottom-up approach that is required, not top-down. So, as Jesus is reported to have said on the cross, "Forgive them, for they do not know", certainly still holds true today.

Falsehoods and misinformation have increased in the modern digital age, so each day it is becoming more of a necessity to discern what we are being fed as news, information and knowledge. For all the wonderful entertainment and learning opportunities the internet offers, there is also an onslaught of opinion, useless information and veiled and blatant lies. What value is the bewildering amount of bizarre, idiotic and time-wasting content to an enquiring mind? The so-called influencers that self-publicise or promote themselves and their sponsored products are certainly affecting the people who spend hours a day watching and, in some cases, emulating these web celebrities. Again, any intellectual nourishment is debatable.

This bombardment of conflicting information and behaviours can lead to increased stress for children and adults alike, as they struggle with identity, setting unachievable standards and information overload. The growing mental health problem will not be solved by government intervention, filtering or censoring. It has to come from educating children (and adults) about self-worth, understanding themselves and seeing beyond or letting go of the noise surrounding every waking minute. This, married with a general education that includes personal well-being and how to truly learn – covering areas such as how to get a good night's sleep, healthy eating, being a true friend, effective communication, stress relief, where to go for accurate information and who you can trust – must be the way forward, for the next generation to survive this assault on their psychological equilibrium.

When two people meet

Whenever two people meet there are really six people present. There is each person as they see themselves, each person as the other person sees them and each person as they truly are.

Life as a mirror

Taking your *Life CV* from *The South* section, look at the ailments, traumas, significant problems or dramas you have had throughout your life. If you think of more, don't forget to add them to your *Life CV*. Can you find positives that have come from each one of them? What has the issue, event or person taught you about yourself?

This mirroring is a common theme in spiritual work. What you give out will come back to you. Negative thoughts and words sent out to another person, for example, may return to bite you in one way or another. In fact, just being in a negative frame of mind can have a detrimental effect on your day. We have all experienced this when, for example, we wake up in a bad mood (maybe due to something that happened the day or night before), stub our toe, spill the coffee, burn the toast, are stuck in traffic and subsequently late for work. The day may continue similarly as we argue with a colleague, miss an important call and forget to pick up the dry cleaning, eventually writing it off as a bad day.

Conversely, a positive start to the day can energise us and help create (see next section) a good day to follow. A morning meditation, prayer, affirmation or a generally optimistic outlook when we first awaken can positively kick-start the day. Practising this regularly can lead to longer periods of good days, resulting in a more stable, clearer and calmer emotional state overall.

Dropping the ego to allow space for creation

Our thoughts create our reality. If in a negative mood, then what we create will likely reflect this. If we can be peaceful, content and feel balanced when we go about our day, the creation impulses will be more positive. What often drives this negative or positive tug of war is our ego. That part of us that wants to be in control, that knows what is best and what is right according to *the law of us*. The ego is influenced by many factors and shaped from an early age, continuing to be our core self until we do something about it. If we don't, the ability to see things differently, embrace empathy and understand another's point of view diminishes. We then only take on board, seek out or connect with what feeds our ego – that which we already agree with. Anything outside of this is dismissed. Some may call this character or personality, but where is the space for change, and how do you go about it? Below are some ways to shatter your ego, provided by Daniel Whalen, NLP Master Practitioner:[20]

- Kill the addiction to approval.
- Seek out praise for others.
- Let go of the false power of anger.
- Spend time alone in nature.
- Be still.
- Use irritation from others as a mirror for yourself.
- Give in to vulnerability.
- Suppress the need to add your opinion to everything
- Question why you do what you do.
- Locate yourself in others as often as possible.

Many of the exercises within this book have been about looking inwards and reflecting on your nature. In a way, they are holding a mirror up to your ego and asking, 'Is this truly me?'

---

[20] *13 Little But Powerful Ways To Shatter Your Ego*, Daniel Whalen, *Neuro–Linguistic Programming (NLP) Master Practitioner, Thoughtcatalog.com*, 7/6/2018.

Other ways to reduce the ego effect are:

- Be in the flow. Do things you love.

- Practice meditation and mindfulness.

- Feel gratitude and compassion. Use gratitude stones.

- Embrace childhood innocence. Nurture your inner child.

- Foster humility. Go on a pilgrimage to a religious or natural site.

Ikigai : **Your reason for being**

Ikigai is a Japanese concept relating to a person's reason for living and can be seen as the convergence of four primary elements:

What you Love (your passion)
What you are Good at (your vocation)
What the World Needs (your mission)
What you can get Paid for (your profession)

Draw your own version of the overlapping circles of the *ikigai* symbol below and consider the following:

- *What do you love?* What aspects of your life bring you into your heart and make you come alive?

- *What are you good at?* What unique skills do you have that come most naturally to you? What talents have you cultivated, and what do you excel at, even when you aren't trying? What is your medicine?

- *What cause do you believe in?* What breaks your heart or pulls at your gut? What change would you most love to create in the world? What would you give your life for?

- *What do people value and pay you for?* What service, value or offering do you bring, or could you bring, that is of real value to others? Something people need and are happy to pay for or share something in exchange?

Write whatever keywords, phrases and ideas come up for you in each circle, then look for areas of natural overlap. Are any of these elements related to each other? The space in the middle is where your *ikigai* resides. Spend time contemplating or meditating as to what this could be. Is there one thing you could do to help this expression of your *ikigai*?

Vision or dream board

Create a collage of your dreams and wishes using glossy magazine pictures, photos, newspaper images or any picture or symbol representing what you want from life. Arrange these on a board, ensuring the images are connected, touching or overlapping. Keep it in a prominent place so that you see it every day, looking at the pictures and visualising your dreams in a slightly more tangible way.

Look for any linkages or themes. What is this vision telling you about yourself? Is this really you, or are you wishing from a place of lack? Do you want something you have been told you should desire? For example, a steady job, long-term relationship, three-bed house, two children, nice car, etc.? These may be true for you, but allow yourself total freedom to dream as wildly and grandly, or as specifically and humbly as you wish.

Update the board regularly as your dreams change or evolve.

Dream journal

Keep a journal by your bed, or use the voice recorder function on your phone to record your dreams. This is easier said than done, as they can often disappear in a moment once we begin to awaken. The trick is to stay with the dream once you have come out of it. Try not to move or open your eyes and take time to review the dream, crystallising the main points in your now semi-awake mind, before making the conscious effort to awaken fully and record the dream.

It has been said that dreams are a method by which the soul is attempting to talk to us. Or maybe it is our subconscious. Perhaps they are similar or the same. However, the language of dreams can be challenging to interpret and the metaphors not obvious. Look for patterns in dreams, especially ones that repeat, but take the explanations for dreams available in books or the internet with a pinch of salt. Use your discernment to understand any meaning.

Affirmations

An affirmation is the reciting of inspirational and aspirational words that resonate with you. It is a positive reinforcement of who you are and who you want to be. Your own mantra. It should be written by yourself, making it personal and pertinent. Use positive, expansive, self-affirming and energising words.

Write the affirmation as though it is your truth and how you currently behave, even if you feel you do not openly show these behaviours. Write it with confidence. Do not use doubtful wording such as "maybe", "if", "I hope that...", etc. Use positive statements, such as "I am", "I know" or "It is". It may seem like an essay the first time around, but once you have the outline, refine it to a powerful core affirmation. Write your affirmation clearly, maybe with an artistic flare, by adding colour, calligraphic swirls, pictures or your symbol (from the *Create your symbol* section).

Keep your affirmation out in the open and read it every day, in the morning and evening. Read it out loud, saying it to yourself in a mirror. Look into your eyes and believe what you are saying. If there is doubt or you feel silly or stupid, look at the reason why? Are these simply not your words? Does something not feel right? If the affirmation is reasonable, something within you is often the issue. Look at the reason for this block, using one of the exercises from previous chapters to unearth and transmute it.

A quick online search will throw up many affirmation examples, but a few are given here:

> *"I surrender to all life has to offer and am excited by the adventure ahead. I am confident in my abilities and trust I will be helped and supported in all my endeavours. I know how to make decisions and am ready to deepen my relationship with spirit and the Universe."*

> *"I am an intelligent, caring and empathic woman, confident in my abilities, happily independent and compassionate to all I meet. I know how beautiful I am and how much love is in my heart."*

Or from Sue Stone's book *Love Life, Live Life:*[21]

> *"I trust in the power and magic of the Universe.*
> *I believe in miracles, miracles happen to me.*
> *I have more love, happiness and abundance in my life than I ever imagined possible."*

Take a photo of what you have written with your phone, so you can refer to it throughout the day, leaving the original in a prominent place at home. You could use your symbol or a talisman as a reminder of this affirmation.

Pioneer / frontier spirit

We do not have to be physically exploring a new place, clambering up a mountain or diving to the depths of an ocean to be a pioneer. 99.9% of species that have ever existed are now extinct, but humans

[21] Sue Stone, *Love Life, Live Life, 2010, Piatkus.*

have survived (and evolved) to be here at this moment in time. Each of us is standing at the forefront of human evolution. We are breathing rarefied air and can look to embrace this pioneer spirit, even if, at times, we feel stuck or unmotivated due to life pressures, government propaganda and control, or media negativity.

What frontiers do you want to push? What knowledge has been hidden from you? What nagging doubts do you have about life as you see it or how it has been presented to you? What doesn't sit right or seem to fit? What cultures, other than your own, can you learn from? What wisdom is out there awaiting you? What piece (or pieces) of the jigsaw are missing for you? It may seem simpler and arguably easier to follow the flock and go along with what society expects, but why not step outside of your comfort zone? Go where there is resistance. Face the fear and do it anyway!

Exploring exercise

When in a new place, maybe on holiday or a day trip, you will be unfamiliar with the area and not know your way around, so you head out and explore. The first time you venture out on foot in this new place, a strong focus is kept on remembering the way back. You look around but always with one eye on the return journey and therefore probably don't take everything in. On the second outing, the route is known and time can be taken for sightseeing. You try another route the third time out, confident you know the area well enough to find your way back. With phones and GPS, the chances of getting lost are slim, but even though this is not in the jungle, on a mountain or under the sea, this is still exploring.

This sense of exploring can be translated to spiritual exercises. Wariness and insecurity on the first attempt, understanding on the second and confidence after that, whenever the exercise is practised. This is one of the many reasons a journal is important; revisiting your notes and the activities attempted to see if you can go a little *off-map*.

And speaking of maps, the maps we are most familiar with provide us with a detailed scaled overview of the land, containing symbols and graphical representations of the real world to help us navigate on a journey. They provide a bigger picture, typically an overhead view, looking down on the area. Maps can be used to get from one place to another, but provide much more information than just a route. Geographical features such as green spaces, rivers, coastlines, forests and contour lines identifying hills and valleys are usually shown. Places of interest are often highlighted and can be included as stop-offs during a journey. Seeing an overall picture of an area may throw up new ideas on where to go and help pick a route that includes visiting the coast, crossing a particular river or passing through a picturesque village for lunch.

Such geographical and road maps are two types of map, but there are many others, such as weather, historical, time zone, habitat, population, climate, political, economic, resource, tourist, nautical, the night sky or even a map of the brain and the neural hotspots within. There are also mind maps to organise information so linkages between sometimes disparate subjects can be revealed.

All maps give a bigger picture and show how the individual parts connect and relate to the whole. With the advent of GPS tracking, real-time maps can show the movements of tagged animals, traffic congestion and, more subversively, the movement of people carrying mobile phones, which nowadays is almost everyone.

When journeying or meditating, we often go to the same or similar places in our minds – places that feel safe or powerful and where we meet spiritual allies or helpers. Mapping this inner landscape, by literally drawing it out on paper, may be helpful in understanding your own psyche. The *Life CV* and *vision board* exercises described in this book are two other ways to produce personal maps, by mapping your past and dreams. Creating a map is a wonderful learning tool and, in itself, exploratory.

The advent of modern technology has somewhat detracted from the sense of exploration when travelling to new places. Mobile phones have taken away the need to observe and take in our surroundings, as wherever we are, our position can be pinpointed on a digital map and a taxi or similar requested to take us home. Being overly reliant upon technology has moved us a little further from our connection to nature and, in this case, traditional ways of navigating and exploring. It is worth trying to get lost, just once in a while, to rekindle that pioneer and explorer feeling within.

Mother Earth - **Our relationship to the environment and all life on this planet**

"Now is the time to give back to Pachamama, Mother Earth. Now is the time for reconnecting to her."
Message from the Q'ero people.

Connection has been referred to often in this book and there is none more profound than our connection to the planet we live upon and the life we share it with. The Earth is our home and, currently, our only home. It is not part of this book's remit to go into the issues of climate change, species extinction, habitat loss, population growth, food quality, clean air and water, or other environmental challenges, but they are problems we are all facing, one way or another.

That said, I believe the two most important factors over the coming years will be **transparency** and **sustainability** in all we do at every level of society. If companies and governments are open and honest in their business and our endeavours: individually, corporately, governmentally and culturally, are sustainable from the point of view of resource use and environmental impact, then the crisis we face may be surmounted.

It will take visionary and revolutionary individuals (leaders, creators and implementers) in all areas of life to move our culture forward to where the future looks bright for us and our children's children. We should have faith in people, in young people especially. If they are offered the proper education, the right tools to apply to problems and the chance to use their creative abilities, then beneficial change and a more positive future is within our grasp.

The Earth is in a constant state of flux: of death and rebirth, mutation and transformation. Nothing is static. Convection currents in the molten iron outer core at the heart of our planet generate a global magnetic field shaped by the Earth's rotation. This magnetic field protects us from harmful solar radiation by deflecting incoming charged particles from the sun. It also helps animals with an evolved sensory capability to navigate in their daily lives, or guide them on an annual migration of hundreds, sometimes thousands, of miles.

The ebb and flow of the oceans, the warming and cooling of land and water, the movement of air, cloud formation and weather systems are all in a continual state of motion and change. On the other hand, we, as sentient, conscious mammals, struggle with change. We can become set in our ways – creatures of habit, comfortable with the familiar or fearful of the unknown, strange and different. Change is seen as a challenge rather than the natural occurrence it is.

The diversity of life and the abundance and variety of environments on Earth is staggering. We can only be left awe-struck when glimpsing even a tiny fraction of the natural world. Mother nature's inherent magnificence and beauty can soon be forgotten when much of our time is spent within similar four-walled boxes: home, school, shops or work. Or when travelling in a box (by road, rail or in the air), looking at one rectangular screen or another, staring out at other rectangular boxes (some towering high and blocking out the natural light), and even lying on a rectangular bed or sofa staring up at a rectangular ceiling, perhaps in expectation of some form of inspiration. It must be difficult to see beyond our compartmentalised lives at times, to see the wonder of nature, the beauty of life and the miracles that occur constantly. Miracles that are, in fact, natural happenings; things that mother nature has been doing for hundreds, thousands and maybe millions of years.

So to help ourselves, we need to ensure our connection to the planet remains strong or, if diminished, is reignited and reinforced. The fears and misnomers about nature and man's relationship to nature – how we must master it, overcome it, defeat it – must be seen as the fearful, indoctrinated views of a time long since passed.

Those that live in harmony with nature accept that they are part of the natural landscape. Indigenous peoples, folk with livelihoods centred around the land and the increasing number of people choosing to return to nature in one way or another, all acknowledge this connection. They understand that nature is not to be bent to their will but a partner to be understood, respected and cherished. To be worked with, not against. They know they are in stewardship of the land rather than ownership, looking after it for future generations.

You do not have to go off-grid or become a sustainable farmer to develop this natural relationship. Simple actions can rekindle this connection with Mother Nature, such as keeping house plants or herbs on the windowsill, composting organic waste, growing fruit and veg, re-purposing outdoor spaces to attract insects and birds or providing food and water for animals. Also, improving your home's energy efficiency, being conscious of the food you buy and eat, and reducing the amount of water wasted benefit a more sustainable lifestyle. Again, numerous books and online resources are available, relating to sustainable, natural living and its positive effects on your wellbeing. However, the following by Isabel Losada[22] summarises what we, as individuals, can do.

"We do need to be radical. We need to change the way that we live – in every way. It's about living lives that are designed to support the Earth. And it can be done in ways that enhance our lives too. Life is short, and we have a planet to save."

---

[22] Isabel Losada, article on climate crisis in The Guardian online newspaper, 4th Nov 2022.

She suggests (and I have expanded a little upon) the following:

- *Leave your High Street bank.* Your loyalty is misplaced. They don't have their lending and investment portfolio in the public domain and are almost certainly supporting the fossil fuel industry. Move to a transparent and reasonably ethical bank. For example, Triodos Bank UK has been voted both 'Best Ethical Financial Provider' and 'Best Investment Provider' at the British Bank Awards 2022.

- *Be a little bit activist.* You don't have to stop traffic, chain yourself to a fence or take roost up a tree, but do something that shows you are not happy with how things are. Be the change you want to see. Support the groups and people trying to do good for the planet: The RSPB, Rewilding Britain, Greenpeace, Fridays for Future, Extinction Rebellion, sign The Fossil Fuel Non-Proliferation Treaty, etc.

- *Switch to an ethical energy company.* Or try not to use their energy at all, by installing solar panels or a wind/water turbine. Make your home as efficient as possible. Insulate. Turn off heating in rooms not in use. Don't overfill your kettle. Hang heavy curtains in winter.

- *Learn the skills of sustainability and self-sufficiency and be creative in how you use them.* You don't have to live exactly like Tom and Barbara in "The Good Life", but they did get a few things right. Bake, pickle and preserve. Eat organic and UK produced foods. Eat healthily and not to excess. Enjoy the simple (and good) life without the necessity for more technology or gadgets. Use handmade items, crafted with love, not plastic.

- *Reuse, re-purpose and recycle.* Make the clothes you own last. Repair worn items. Learn to mend, to sew, knit or crotchet. Buy second-hand clothes or sustainable, well-made items that will last. Repair and restore furniture. Move items around to change the space, rather than totally redecorate or buy new.

- *Restrict national flights and only take a foreign holiday once a year.* Swap your car for public transport or a bike. Walk more, noticing and enjoying the neighbourhood you are passing through.

I believe we, as humans, have the energies of the planet at our disposal. The animals and plants, the waterways and air, the soil and land, all available to use, commune with and work with spiritually, helping us understand and strengthen this primeval connection. The medicine plants, ancient trees, flowing waterfalls, rocks, crystals and every other natural resource can have significance for us on our journey through life, and play their part in forming our internal and external landscape.

Plant medicines

The term plant medicine is used to cover all products produced from plantlife to treat disease or help with health. In this section, I am specifically referring to the psychoactive plants used in shamanic cultures for healing work. To most Westerners, these plant medicines are not medicines but 'drugs' and, if illegal, to be avoided, deemed dangerous and anyone who takes or *uses* them condemned. These are not plant medicines. These are recreational drugs, perhaps experimented with initially when an adolescent and sometimes used more regularly in adulthood, often as an escape. Yes, there can be progression onto more potent and addictive substances, possibly resulting in wrecked lives and even death, but this is not the inevitable path for most who try recreational drugs. Of course, legal drugs such as tobacco and alcohol are deemed acceptable by society, even though they cause more harm than probably any other form of legal or illegal recreational drug.

All medicines have come from nature originally. Their active ingredients isolated from the plant, fungi, tree or other organic matter in a lab, chemically replicated and mass-produced in pill or potion form. No doubt, for the majority of people, prescribed medication has helped. But this is too often only a way to treat the symptoms, not the underlying cause. Prescribed drugs may also have physical and psychological side effects, possibly affecting mental health. For example, the often cited side effects of anti-depressants are an emotional numbing of the patient and a feeling of detachment from life.

The healing effect of plant medicines is beginning to be recognised by Western medicine, with continuing research being conducted by various respected bodies, including the Psychedelic Trials Group, King's College London and the Centre for Psychedelic Research, Imperial College London. The latter have promising results from a recent trial using psilocybin (the active ingredient in magic mushrooms) to help treat clinical depression.[23]

From a shamanic perspective, plant medicines are gifts from *Mother Earth*. They are cultivated and prepared by the shaman or shamanic practitioner in a sacred way, with the spirit of the plant honoured and the potent healing properties respected. When plant medicines are used, it is within the framework of a ceremony (and not recreationally), often with days or weeks of preparation by the individual beforehand, possibly including abstinence from alcohol, sex and drugs, eating a natural and cleansing diet, and spending time in meditation readying oneself.

[23] David Nutt, David Erritzoe, Robin Carhart-Harris, *Psychedelic Psychiatry's Brave New World*, Cell volume 181 Issue 1, 02/04/2020.

Plant medicines are an important part of shamanic and indigenous cultures and a vibrant natural way to connect to non-ordinary reality. They also afford a method to supercharge the imagination and *see* in the mind, especially helpful if one finds visualising difficult.

Personally, I do not feel that plant medicines are necessary to live a spiritual life. Still, if you venture deeper into shamanism or nature-based spirituality they will be encountered and, quite naturally, you would want to experience their potent effects. However, I strongly suggest that plant medicines should not be a direct *go-to* for spiritual enlightenment or a vacation add-on but rather used only after a period of working on yourself (such as via the exercises in this book) to uncover and clear many of your blocks and issues.

Note: Safety warning
If you choose to take plant medicines, you need to be aware of their legality, which varies from country to country. Also, I strongly suggest only taking them in a formalised ceremony under the guidance of a qualified shaman or shamanic practitioner you trust (and have known long enough to build trust with), in a place where you feel safe and secure, and with a group you feel comfortable sharing the experience with.

Working with plant medicines can be traumatic if you do not know what you are doing, so you need to place your trust in those conducting the ceremony.

There will always be negative stories around such activities, but the vast majority of shamans and shamanic practitioners honour the sacredness of the work they have been called to undertake, and hold safe, loving ceremonies to help heal their communities.

General connecting and balancing visualisation

When out in nature, take a moment to stop, close your eyes and breathe in the life force all around. Slow down and connect with the sounds and smells, letting the energy of the place flow in and out with your breath. Feel alive with all your senses.

The following visualisation takes this further, connecting you to all there is and helping to clear blockages and fill gaps from any perceived loss, bringing you back into a healthy balance.

All life came from the stars. Atoms of matter created during or soon after the Big Bang have formed and reformed over billions of years, been transformed and transmuted in generation after generation of star formation, recycled and redistributed when the stars turn supernova and explode. Almost five billion years ago, after more than a thousand generations of these stellar formations, our star, the Sun, was birthed. Subsequently, Earth and the other planets within the Solar System coalesced into being.

Over time, the atmosphere, land and seas formed on our planet, with the first life appearing around three billion years ago. The heat, light and invisible (to humans) electromagnetic radiation produced by the Sun fuelled the development of the first organisms, and continues to be the building block of all life on Earth. We are connected to everything through this process of stellar evolution. Connected to all that has been and all that will be, by the Sun.

Relax and allow your breathing to slow. Ideally, be outside on a sunny day where you can safely feel the Sun on your face, otherwise, imagine the Sun's rays beaming down upon you.

Begin by focusing on the Sun in your mind. Travel out in space and be in front of it. Feel, as best you can, its enormity and power. Let it blast through you, vaporise you, dismantle you completely, annihilating every molecule, every atom. Then allow the disintegrated mist that is *you* to drift through space and be scattered across the planet. Feel as though *you* cover the entire Earth, becoming part of the oceans, evaporating into clouds, falling as rain, into lakes, streams and rivers and flowing back to the sea. Feel yourself mingle with the atmosphere and become the air every plant and leaf takes in, the air every animal and human breathes.

Breathe in knowing you are linked to everything; breathe out knowing whatever has left you goes to connect with everything outside of you. Continue to bring the inner and outer into balance. Everything is in you; you are in everything. Visualise your energy body, allowing blockages to dissipate and voids to be filled. Repeat the mantra "I am one with the Universe, the Universe is one with me" or "I am one with God (or spirit), God (or spirit) is one with me." Find balance in this cycle of breathing everything in and out.

Note: The number of atoms in the human body is seven octillion (7×10^{27} - a seven with twenty-seven zeros after it). Planet Earth is 510 trillion (510×10^{12}) square metres in total surface area (land and sea), so if your body was vaporised into a wind of atoms that were scattered upon the whole of the earth's surface, then the maths works out at around 13 trillion (13×10^{12}) atoms of *you* per square metre. This clearly means that there would be a vast part of *you* everywhere and *you* would most definitely be part of everything. If you replace atoms for the much larger human cell in which they reside (and containing the building block of life, DNA), then this still works out at around a dozen cells per square metre across the whole surface of the planet. Knowing this may help with the visualisation.

Strip away exercise

As a thought experiment, visualise where you live with everything artificial removed. Imagine it as it was pre-industrial revolution. Just humans and nature in a simple symbiotic, bountiful and peaceful relationship. Ignore thoughts around any difficulties living, disease, famine, natural disasters, etc. Visualise only living in peace. Living comfortably off the land and being content. Remember how simple it was to live with the necessary resources around us and the teachings required, passed down from generation to generation. Connect again with the energy of these teachings, a wisdom based on nature. Now bring these feelings of healthy, content and symbiotic living back to your current life. Feel how they are still prevalent and pertinent in this world with all its technology, gadgets, systems and man-made constructions. Acknowledge that this knowledge still has value, and is available to us if we work with our natural state and create space for it. This natural connection can soon be rekindled by spending time in nature, away from the city's frenetic activity and urban life.

Trees and wood

You start as a seedling - hold on tight.
The will of creation, free to take flight.
Imagine your roots, extending deep underground.
Your branches spreading out, reaching for stars that abound.
Feel grounded and strong, growing towards the light.
Welcome sheltering creatures, on a wet, windy night.
Stand proud in your majesty; a family tree for the ages.
Know your wisdom is shared, within some wood-pulped pages.

Trees have naturally been mentioned many times in this book, which is unsurprising, knowing their value to the natural world and to us as humans. Their significance can only be touched upon in these pages as their usefulness is seemingly unending: as providers of oxygen, fire for warmth, security and cooking, building materials, food, medicines, rubber, incense and resins, to play upon as children, shelter under out of the rain, doze against in the shade on a summer's afternoon or even climb up into out of a predator's reach! Wood can be carved into bowls and spoons, made into furniture, artwork or toys, transformed into paper and books, fashioned into tools, arrows or spears or simply used as a walking stick. It is no surprise that trees, and the wood they provide, are so revered.

It is not only for practical reasons that the tree is so loved. Spiritually too, it plays its role. The tree has always been linked to spiritual metaphor: growing tall and strong from a tiny seed, anchoring roots deep into the earth and spreading its bows heavenwards, absorbing carbon dioxide and 'breathing out' oxygen; and in the case of the oak during its leafless winter months, looking almost like the brachia of human lungs.

This above and below metaphor – the duality of life – is encapsulated in a tree. From the outset, humanity is split into male and female. Half the world's population are women, half men. Duality is a given: night and day, on and off, left and right, up and down, male and female, as above, as below. Why should it be any different when it comes to a spiritual outlook on life? This duality persists. In the form of an upward or above, spiritual connection, coupled with a downward or lower, soul connection.

As Bill Plotkin highlights in his book *Soulcraft:*[24]

> *"Spirit connection above, soul purpose below... Soul embraces and calls us toward what is most unique in us. Spirit encompasses and draws us toward what is most universal and shared."*

Reaching for the sky while rooted to the earth, trees show us the above and the below coming together as one. An excellent representation of the human spiritual journey. Sending roots down in discovery of the soul, creating a strong foundation for the trunk of core growth, which supports the desire to extend upwards, and connect to what is beyond and out of reach – perhaps even connecting to all that is. This symbolism, married with the evident natural connection, is why the tree is often used for shamanic or spiritual journeying work as the *axis mundi* for spiritual exploration: embarking on a lower-world journey via the roots or hollow in the tree, taking us downwards, or climbing the trunk and branches skywards, propelling us towards the upper world.

With all its uses, particularly as a building material for shelter and fuel for heating and cooking, wood was historically seen as being more than just useful, but essential. Not having wood to cook with or warm a shelter would clearly be a disastrous situation, while conversely, having an abundance of wood could be seen as fortunate, perhaps even lucky to some degree. Knocking on wood or using the phrase "touch wood", reflects this. Moreover, the feel of wood, by hugging a tree, sitting at a wooden table or holding a stick, is grounding. It provides a connection to something natural and to Mother Nature in general. Compare holding something wooden to something plastic, for example.

---

[24] Bill Plotkin, *Soulcraft*, 2003, New World Library.

There is also the artistic element of wood that gives it value. The colour, shapes, textures and patterns created by the grain, and the way it wears over time, its patina, revealing a history of use, and often becoming more visually beautiful with age.

Try cultivating your relationship with trees and wood. What trees do you know? Which ones are native to your country or area? Use wood in your hobbies. Carve a spoon, construct a spice rack or bird box, fashion a staff or walking stick. Make a conscious effort to touch and feel anything wooden. Choose wood over artificial materials in your home for your furniture, especially tables. Reclaim, restore and re-purpose wooden items. Touch and feel the bark of a tree. Say hello to a tree, even hug one. Wander your neighbourhood and take in all the trees around you. Spot the tallest or largest tree in a group. Research is now discovering that this is often a 'grandmother tree'. One that looks after any local tree in distress by communicating with the underground fungal network via her roots, and sending out helpful water and nutrients. The 2019 study, *Protect Oak Ecosytems*[25] [sadly started in response to an acute decline of oak trees within the UK], showed that native oaks are home to some 2,300 separate species, with over five hundred completely dependent or highly reliant upon the oak. So next time you look at an oak, realise it is more than just a tree, but a whole ecosystem of lifeforms living together and calling the tree their home.

Trees have stood through the centuries, survived lightning strikes and disease, and have grown to be one of the largest living organisms on Planet Earth. General Sherman, a Giant Sequoia in the Sequoia National Park, California, USA, is around 2,500 years old and thought to weigh approximately two-thousand tonnes. The national park is full of these incredible trees and hiking in the area

---

[25] Their website: protectouroaks.wordpress.com

truly feels like walking amongst giants. California must be a good climate for trees, as nearby in the White Mountains is a bristle cone pine that is believed to be the oldest living organism on the planet, standing tall for some 5,000 years.

Trees, and the forests they thrive within, have been stable natural havens much longer than a few thousand years. In fact, rainforests are the oldest ecosystems on Earth. Some can trace their origins back to 70 million years ago, when dinosaurs roamed the planet – the rainforest of Borneo is thought to be around a staggering 130 million years old.

If trees could speak, what stories they could tell. They rightly have a special place in our hearts, and we must do all we can to ensure that these 'tall standing ones' survive and flourish for the benefit of future generations.

Create your own talking stick or wand

A talking stick is sometimes used in groups when sitting in council or sharing. It is passed around, signifying whose turn it is to speak while all others listen in silence. A talking stick gives the holder permission (and the authority) to compose themselves, speak from the heart and take their time talking, without fear of interruption. Using a wooden stick provides something natural and tangible to hold while collecting thoughts, and can be a focal point if speaking the words is a struggle. It can be held loosely and gesticulated when in full flow or held tightly and hit on the ground if deeper emotion comes with what has to be said. Passing the stick around the group (usually sitting in a circle) gives a chance for every person present to speak; not only the loudest or most self-confident. All can and should be heard, as everybody has some wisdom to share.

This, I believe, is partly the origin of wands. We look at magic, the occult, witches and wizards with much scepticism in the modern world. But take yourself back to a time when we were living with a more profound connection to the land. When trees and the wood they provided were honoured as the essential resource they were. It is then not too difficult to comprehend the development of such magical sticks.

Make your own talking stick or wand by finding a piece of wood about 30cm (12 inches) in length that feels right in your hand. Ensure it is strong enough to withstand being held tightly and resist snapping. Trim and carve it with a knife, removing any shoots, bumps or ridges along the stick's length, leaving enough texture as is your preference and ensuring there are no sharp edges or prongs on the ends.

You can use this stick in ceremonial work: as a talking stick, to wave as a wand, draw on the ground, tap on various parts of your body to help emotional release or simply to hold and feel a connection to nature. Keeping it on or near your altar will help reinforce its potency and usefulness.

Be a tree

Ideally, do this exercise on the earth with bare feet. If not possible, visualise yourself standing barefoot on the land.

Imagine and visualise roots coming out from the soles of your feet. Allow these roots to spread and go deep into the earth, visualising them twisting and turning through the soil and into the rock, maybe through air pockets or caves deep underground. Then extend your arms out and up, like the branches of a tree, and look skywards.

Breathe in and visualise sunlight and heavenly energy entering through your hands, arms and face, and into your torso. As you breathe out, send this energy through your torso and legs, out of your feet and down your roots into the earth. Maybe *see* the energy as a colour. Now, reverse the process. This time, on the in-breath, bring life force energy up from the earth, through your roots, into your feet and up into your entire body. Then, on the out-breath, see it flow out of your head and outstretched arms into the Universe. Repeat this cycle, flushing yourself with alternate Universal and Earth energy, until you feel cleansed, recharged and balanced.

Some tai-chi, qi-gong and yoga movements are based on this tree symbolism and metaphor.

Sit under a tree

Trees can act as antennas. They were used as such in the Vietnam war and since by electronics hobbyists. Trees can also be spiritual antennas, allowing us to commune with nature and our inner selves. The Buddha is said to have achieved enlightenment while meditating under a bodhi (fig) tree. So why not try this for yourself? Your experience may not be quite so *mind-blowing*, but still worth the effort. Sit under a tree with your back to the trunk and connect with the 'spirit' of the tree. Close your eyes or let your gaze soften. Commune with the tree. Ask it questions. Allow the answers to come to you in your imagination or as a message from nature, such as an animal appearing, an unexpected sound or perhaps resonating words from an overheard conversation between passers-by.

The plaque on the bench my father made in memory of my mother, who passed in 1998, says: "To be close to me, just sit by a tree."

Belly button stick

The belly button, or navel, is the attachment point for the umbilical cord, through which, while in the womb, we received the energy and nutrients necessary to grow from our mother via the placenta. Revisit this connection by taking a small stick, about two centimetres (one inch) in diameter, and holding it into or onto your belly button while gently tapping it with another stick. Feel the vibration and bring your focus to your mother. What emotions or feelings arise doing this?

Try using a long stick to connect your belly button directly to the earth. Tap this longer stick. Again, feel the vibration, but this time dwell on the connection being made to *Mother Earth.*

Fungi

Fungi are classified separately from other lifeforms as, from a scientific perspective, they are not part of the plant or animal kingdoms. Their differences and usefulness have only recently begun to be unearthed, showing there is more to these organisms than perhaps first thought. We now know that only the fruiting part of the fungus is visible, while the organism's main body lies hidden underground. The mycelium, as this is termed, forms part of an underground communication network between many, if not all, of the local plant life. This *wood-wide-web* acts as a passageway for the trees and plants to swap nutrients, electrical signals and chemical messages. With trillions of end branchings, there are thought to be over 300 miles of these fungal threads under every footstep you take on the land, locking in vast amounts of carbon underground.[26] The healing effect of mushrooms and the active ingredients some contain

---

[26] From *Fantastic Fungi*, a film by Louis Schwartzberg, 2019.

has been touched upon in the *plant medicines* section, and their use as a nutrient-rich food source is common knowledge, even if their texture is not to everybody's liking.

Richard Gray's article, *The Unexpected Magic of Mushrooms*[27], highlights more astonishing facts, some of which are summarised below:

> *"Fungi are some of the most common organisms on our planet; the combined biomass of these often tiny organisms exceeds that of all the animals on the planet put together. And we are discovering new fungi all the time. More than 90% of the estimated 3.8 million fungi in the world are currently unknown to science. In 2017 alone, there were 2,189 new species of fungi described by scientists.*
>
> *A recent report published by the UK's Royal Botanic Gardens in Kew, London, highlighted that fungi are already used in hundreds of different ways, from making paper to helping to clean our dirty clothes.*
>
> *Around 15% of all vaccines and biologically produced drugs come from fungi. The complex proteins used to trigger an immune response to the hepatitis B virus, for example, are grown in yeast cells, which are part of the fungi family. Perhaps the most well-known is the antibiotic penicillin, which was discovered in a common type of household mould that often grows on old bread. Dozens of other types of antibiotics are now produced by fungi...*
>
> *...A fungus found growing in soil at a landfill site on the outskirts of Islamabad, Pakistan, may be a solution to the*

---

[27] Richard Gray, *The Unexpected Magic of Mushrooms*, 15/03/19, *BBC future* website.

alarming levels of plastic pollution clogging up our oceans. Fariha Hasan, a microbiologist at Quaid-I-Azam University in Islamabad, discovered that the Aspergillus tubingensis fungus can rapidly break down polyurethane plastic...

...California-based MycoWorks have been developing ways of turning mushrooms into building materials. By fusing wood together with mycelium, they have been able to create bricks that are fire-retardant and tougher than conventional concrete...

...Fungi can also be used in combination with traditional building materials to create a "smart concrete" that can heal itself as the fungi grows into any cracks that form, secreting fresh calcium carbonate, the key raw material in concrete, to repair the damage."

Clearly, our knowledge of these mainly hidden organisms is still in its infancy, with more uses undoubtedly waiting to be unearthed.

Holding history

History is often deduced from small pieces of evidence, such as shards of bone, broken artefacts or fossilised remains. With some rudimentary archaeological, geological or similar historical analysis skills, these items tell a story. That said, you do not need a background in archaeology to connect to the past. We can all do this easily through meditation, visualisation or journeying, and by connecting with nature – especially ancient natural objects such as rocks and stones formed millions of years ago. In the UK, the youngest rocks are about 50 million years old, the oldest around 500 million. Scientists in North America have found rocks believed to be over four billion years old in Hudson Bay, Northern Quebec. Therefore, touching a rock face, sitting on a boulder, picking up a pebble from the beach or holding a crystal is a direct link to the past.

Choose a stone you like, maybe one with special meaning to you and sit with it. Look at it, feel its history. Notice how it has weathered, been eroded over time, or possibly broken off from a much larger piece. If you are in the UK, accept that it is at least 50 million years old. Can you begin to imagine that sort of time? Holding a fossil can have a similar effect, perhaps more so than a rock, as you are holding something that lived millions of years ago.

When out walking, if you see a fern (*Polypodiopsida* genus), stop for a moment and realise that it comes from one of the oldest groups of plants still alive today, dating back to the Devonian period, 400 million years ago. A living fossil. Another is the gingko biloba tree (*gingko* genus). This species of tree has survived since before the age of the dinosaurs, with fossilised leaves discovered over 200 million years old, and almost the same physically as they are now.

Some animals too have changed little over time and are similarly classed as living fossils, such as the horseshoe crab, crocodile, elephant shrew, spectacled bear, giant salamander and the prehistoric-looking coelacanth fish. Connecting with these animals is a direct link to the past, even if it is only through books, TV or the internet. If you are lucky enough to encounter one at a zoo or, more majestically, in the wild, this connection can be pretty humbling.

World water sharing

At a spiritual event I attended some years ago, one of the guest speakers talked about the water he had been collecting from his travels around the globe. For several years he visited most of the planet's oceans and seas, along with many lakes and rivers, collecting water from each. He shared this water with those at the gathering, pouring a little into the plastic bottles we had been asked to bring, so that more people could be part of this wonderfully connecting process.

Mixing and diluting the water does not detract from this connection due to the vast number of water molecules in every drop. In my bottle of world water, a small 18ml (0.6 fl oz) dropper bottle, there are $6x10^{23}$ (a six with twenty-three zeros after it) molecules of H_2O. So even if the water were diluted one million times, it would still contain $6x10^{17}$ molecules of the original water. Therefore, I know my small bottle contains molecules from waterways, streams, ponds, rivers, lakes and seas worldwide.

Continuing to share this water, by putting a few drops into others' empty bottles and topped up with local water, keeps this process alive. Of course, water is in a state of flux across the planet; freezing and melting, condensing and evaporating, and therefore, naturally mixed up. But I still like this idea of world water sharing and the meaningful connection contained in this small bottle.

Offerings

Offerings to the land, deities, spirits and departed loved ones have been given by people throughout history as an act of remembrance and gratitude. If you wish to make an offering, try to keep it relatively small, as it is the gesture that counts, not the size of the offering. Also, ensure it is organic and in keeping with the environment, not permanent or intrusive. For example, as pretty as they are, tying non-biodegradable coloured ribbons to trees is not an offering but rather an egotistical display. The natural world is already so blighted by man's intervention and constructions we should endeavour not to add to this problem.

Nature mandala

When out on the land, create a beautiful mandala or picture out of the natural objects nearby. Choose somewhere that feels right for you or where you notice things you want to touch and arrange in some way. Some people like to balance rocks on the beach; others adorn trees with iconography and messages. Please make sure whatever you use is natural and biodegradable. Open space beforehand if you are drawn to and create a circle with natural items such as leaves, feathers, stones or twigs. Perhaps place rocks in the four cardinal directions or make a cross with twigs and decorate the surroundings as you see fit. Try to avoid picking flowers and plants, and use only what is laying around. Create something beautiful and meaningful to you, in tune with the landscape. Have an intention as you create it, even if it is simply a thank you to *Mother Earth*.

The elements

The four elements of earth, air, fire and water (and sometimes a fifth, metal or aether) have been honoured and respected by all cultures as being the core substances of our planet, pre-dating any scientific knowledge around the periodic table. Nowadays, of course, we realise this is a simplistic view due to the complexity of the chemistry at play. Nonetheless, revering and working spiritually with these elements still offers insight and tangible benefits, especially as we encapsulate them within ourselves; fire as temperature, water as blood, earth as bones and air in our lungs.

We can also look at the elements more esoterically:

- **Earth** - Look to nurture and ground your body: *Feel connected.*

- **Fire** - Burn away the old; stoke the fire of your passions, your heart's calling: *Take action.*

- **Air** - Clear the mind of clutter and negativity; breathe out and let go of what no longer serves you: *Find peace.*

- **Water** - Be in the flow; move with the ebb and tide of your emotions. Take responsibility for how you feel: *Allow movement.*

Throughout this book there are a variety of exercises and visualisations that work with the elements, either individually or together. You may wish to represent each one with an object on your altar that can be useful in meditation or journeying work. Additionally, create an artwork or nature mandala honouring each of the elements or perhaps conduct a ceremony around them.

Fire ceremony

The most obvious element to hold a ceremony around is fire. A real fire can become the focal point and central hub for any group work, but it can also be worked with individually by building a small fire or using a candle. Often we work with fire at twilight or during the hours of darkness, so this lends itself naturally to a more focussed and spiritual connection. Fire is captivating and seemingly alive in how the flames dance, the colours morph and glow, the smoke swirls or the wood crackles, hisses and pops. Additionally, the smell of a wood fire is primordial, a direct link to the past and all fires that have gone before. Personally, I find the smell familiar but mystical;

energising but comforting. If making a real fire, be conscious not to make it too large or waste wood. It should be suited to your or the group's needs.

A fire ceremony can be used for many purposes, depending on your intention. From welcoming in a new moon phase or season, honouring ancestors or mother nature, letting go and asking the fire to transmute negative or unwanted energies, or as a simple prayer to the fire for something positive to manifest.

Remember to open space before lighting the fire and beginning your ceremony. Write down any prayer (for yourself or another) on a piece of paper. When the fire is fully lit, kneel in front of the flames and read your prayer, fully feeling the wishes. Place the paper into the fire and watch it ignite and burn before moving away. You may wish to pull the smoke from the fire into your body – belly, heart or head – to connect physically to the request made. As an alternative to paper, a stick can be used to hold your prayer, maybe decorating it appropriately beforehand, then feeding it to the fire during the ceremony.

Singing, chanting and drumming around the fire are good ways to raise the energy and help break down inhibitions. They can also act as a supporting backing track when each person feeds their prayer to the fire. When all have put their paper or stick onto the fire, slowly allow the song/chant/drumming to come to an end and spend a few moments in silence gazing into the fire. Thank those that attended, any spirits welcomed to the gathering and *Grandfather Fire* for hearing and taking away your prayers.

If in a group, it is a good idea to ask everyone to bring food to share after the fire ceremony, helping ground the energy and fostering a sense of friendship and community. The fire can then be used as any other campfire for sitting around, toasting marshmallows, playing a guitar and having a sing-a-long or softly gazing into.

Natural forces exercises

The forces of nature are breathtaking to behold and often overwhelming with the power they conduct. From lightning storms to volcanic eruptions, tornadoes to earthquakes, tsunamis to wildfires. This power can be tapped into using photos or video footage from the internet for use in your own meditations and journeying work.

Take this further by visualising the most powerful energetic events in the Universe: stars exploding as supernovae, the irresistible pull of a black hole, the energy released in a mass coronal ejection from the Sun or the biggest bang of them all at the beginning of the Universe. These are all natural occurrences that generate mind-boggling energy. Why not harness and use it? If not in reality, then in your imagination. Immerse yourself in this vast energy, knowing you are connected to it.

At the other extreme, the natural world can be used for relaxation, reflection and finding inner-peace. The mist and fog that may appear on a becalmed day can be eerily bewitching and, if walked through, will often lead naturally to spiritual introspection. Listening to audio files of the calming sound of running water, the noise of the wind rustling through the tree tops (known as psithurism), the gentle background chirp of crickets in warmer climates or watching nature-based mindfulness videos can all soothe and nourish your soul.

Memorable pets and animal encounters

We have probably all had pets at some time and been drawn to certain animals in the garden, at the zoo or when seen in a nature documentary. List out these animals and any other animals you had an affinity with as a child, noting the names of pets. Are there any animals you are drawn to currently or ones that keep appearing or popping up?

Animals are often used as helpers in spiritual and, specifically, shamanic and animistic settings. These *power*, *totem* or *spirit animals* are called upon to be with us energetically, to help and teach us something. Often there is a connection to the animal stemming back to our childhood – maybe it was kept as a pet, we were read stories about it, we saw one regularly in our neighbourhood or we had a picture of the animal on our wall.

If time is spent observing animals, it will be noted that each species has its particular traits, abilities and behaviours, all of which can show us lessons helpful in our lives.

For example, the teamwork displayed by a colony of ants is staggering, with each ant seemingly oblivious to any sense of self-preservation or selfish behaviour. Everything each ant does is for the colony. There is no moaning or complaining; they get on and do what nature intended. Altruistic behaviour personified. The patience and stillness of the spider in her web, the acute sight of the hawk, the silence of the owl in flight or the echolocation of the bat all show how wonderfully adapted each of these creatures has become to its environment.

These evolutionary gifts showcase how nature has modified herself over time into the variety and abundance we know today, with the abilities of some within the animal kingdom seemingly magical, as they are so detached from our capabilities.

They are, of course, only natural.

Be an animal

Man has always tried to imitate nature: from singing songs like a nightingale to dressing flamboyantly and strutting proudly like a peacock or bird of paradise – often to impress a potential romantic partner. In modern times, with machinery and technology, we can emulate nature further; the jaguar's growl heard in the guttural throb of an idling V8 engine; the lion's roar when *roaring* away at speed on a motorbike; taking to the skies in a plane, para-glider or wing-suit to explore the realm of the birds soaring high over land and sea.

Shamans work directly with animal spirits, and to help embody the animal further, tribal shamans will often create costumes, head-dresses or jewellery with the animal's feathers, hide or bones. With a little dressing up or applying some make-up, we can also embody the spirit of an animal. If this seems a little extreme, then pretend to be the animal. Be as a child and become the animal. Get on all fours and prowl around like a cat, bark like a dog, howl like a wolf, caw as a crow. Embody this as much as you can, even if you feel uncomfortable. As we age, we often forget our sense of play as expectations and cultural pressures steer us away from childlike innocence and behaviour.

Draw on your inner child work from *The North* section and take a few moments to reconnect to the child inside, letting the spirit of the animal you are mimicking take over. Do this for any animal you are drawn to. Maybe start with your power animal if you have met it.

Remember that you are not limited to land-based animals. Only in recent years have we been able to fly above the clouds and gain our airborne cousins' perspective. Try flying in your imagination, soaring, swooping and diving. Or visualise yourself burrowing underground, digging into the earth, being surrounded by it, cocooned in *Mother Earth*'s womb. Squeeze through tunnels. Be in your warren, your cave, your chamber. Become an aquatic animal and play in the surf or dive to the depths of the oceans, effortlessly moving in all directions that being weightless in water allows.

Play with and explore all of these places in nature, ideally in private, where your inhibitions are lowered, or you may attract some interesting and quizzical looks. The use of a blindfold would be helpful.

Mother Earth healing ceremony

Core to any nature-based spiritual tradition is honouring and offering healing to our planet and all the life she supports. The ceremony outlined here can be adapted as you wish. If you do not have a specific Mother Earth object on your altar, I suggest it is worth finding one. Anything natural that represents nature, a symbolic mother, being nurtured or similar is okay, as long as it encourages you to think of the planet when you hold it.

Create a nature mandala outside or within your home, perhaps on or near your altar. Sit next to your natural picture while holding the *Mother Earth* object from your altar and meditate or journey, sending love and gratitude to the earth. Use a drum, rattle or play an audio file if this helps. Allow your thoughts and the visualisation to become as grand as you can, as powerful as you can. Feel unconditional love radiate from your heart. Sense this heart light healing the planet, wildlife, forests, rivers and oceans. Imagine it bathing sacred sites, transmuting wounds and mending broken relationships. See it bring balance and harmony, connecting to all life. Visualise people as happy and free, ready to fulfil their potential. Love cannot be used up, so generate as much as possible. Allow the energy you have transmitted or channelled to go wherever it is needed, having a positive effect.

When you feel you have done enough, move into gratitude for the gifts you have been given and the positive energy you have shared with the planet. Feel the gratitude and love from a thankful *Mother Earth*, accepting also, that you are worthy to receive such love.

Spend a moment contemplating what actions you can take to continue to help the planet in your everyday life, even if it is just more reusing, repurposing or recycling.

Father Sky - **Connecting with all that is beyond, the Great Mystery**

"The history of humanity has been slowly increasing the boundaries of knowledge, knowing more and more and more, and feeling comfortable inside there, but at the edges it is always going to be a challenge."
Neil Armstrong.

Above us, in the daytime, are the clouds, birds, the Sun and sky. During the night, the stars, planets and Moon shine, slowly traversing over our heads in their captivating starry firmament way. We look to the heavens for inspiration, raise our arms high in exaltation, jubilation and victory. We punch the air when we get a win or a result in whatever endeavour we are engaged in. There is something out of this world (literally) and beyond our reach in the vast space above our heads. Above is far away, untouchable, expansive and aspirational. It is the place of dreams. Quoting Browning again, "Man's reach should exceed his grasp or what's a heaven for."

It seems to be part of our DNA to explore – to be adventurous and make discoveries. This exploration takes many forms, from navigating upstream on jungle rivers, crossing frozen wastes, diving to the ocean depths, rocketing to and stepping upon the lunar surface or sending probes on infinite journeys into outer space.

These outer explorations are easy to understand and relate to. The planning, expertise and resources necessary for these endeavours, coupled with the bravery (perhaps sometimes foolhardiness) and skills of those undertaking the missions, not only helps provide answers to scientific questions, but offers insights into the human psyche and spirit, reinforcing the belief that we, as a species, can achieve anything we set out to achieve.

Inner explorations and examinations of the small are just as worthwhile, but maybe a little more challenging to grasp. Carl Jung suggested a global energetic interconnection when he introduced the term *collective consciousness*, representing a shared unconscious between all of humanity. Taking this further, the field of quantum is beginning to shed new light on previously held conceptions of reality, linking it with the idea of an energy of consciousness. Physicist and self-proclaimed quantum activist, Dr Amit Goswami, says in his book *The Everything Answer Book*:[28]

> *"Consciousness is the energy behind life, a quantum energy. Thoughts can create things from the quantum of potentiality. This links science and religion or spirituality. The Newtonian scientific view is based around particles and waves being separate. Quantum allows both to exist. It is only when observed that the field collapses and either one or the other is seen."*

Is a quantum energy of consciousness the creative force behind spiritual and energetic healing? Is this how we create our reality with thoughts? Maybe such interconnection pervades all life?

Within my shamanic healing work, I offer remote sessions where myself and the client do not have to be in the same room, or even the same country, for that matter. Distance is not a barrier to energetic healing and the powerful transformational effect it can have when a mutual intention is being worked upon. Quantum Entanglement, where particles are seemingly connected, even if

[28] Dr Amit Goswami, *The Everything Answer Book: How Quantum Science Explains Love, Death, and the Meaning of Life, 2017, Hampton Roads Publishing Co.*

separated by a distance, is beginning to explain this scientifically, with Einstein calling it "spooky action at a distance". In my experience, it is not *spooky* but genuine, and significant changes can occur, even if the practitioner and client are in separate locations.

New scientific discoveries are continually being made, reinforcing that, as a species, we still have much to learn. At CERN, the international scientific research facility in Switzerland, the Large Hadron Collider (LHCb) is being used to try and unlock some of the mysteries of the Universe. The scientists are looking to build upon The Standard Model that describes all the known fundamental particles (including the exotically named quarks, fermions, hadrons, leptons and the infamous Higgs Boson) underpinning the fabric of the Universe. New particles are being discovered all the time with, in 2018 alone, fifty-nine new hadrons and four tetraquarks added to the list.

Then there are the questions of dark energy and dark matter. What is this energy and material necessary to balance the equations of the observable universe? We are told that the Universe comprises 85% dark matter. If true, how much do we know about the bigger picture of our universe? Clearly, we do not know it all and never will, because science will always lag behind *what is*. As discussed at the beginning of this book, *what is* is *what is*. It is everything. *What is* includes the laws of nature, those we know and have put names and equations to, but also those we currently do not know or only have theories about.

As I write this, the NASA probe New Horizons is flying past Pluto at the outer reaches of our solar system, showing us how far man has come scientifically. Even with such great strides, there are still numerous questions waiting to be fully answered by science, such as the previously mentioned question of dark matter and dark energy, the existence of extra-terrestrial life, how to cure illnesses, a better understanding of how the brain works, what is junk DNA for, what is anti-matter and what other exotic energies will the science of quantum throw up to add to The Standard Model?

I'm sure science will eventually answer these questions or at least lead us toward the answers. In contrast, shamanism and nature-based spiritual philosophies, have been able to circumvent the need for answers, as at their core is a connection to the web of life – an energetic link to all life on the planet and a knowing that they are an intrinsic part of an ever-changing universe, working symbiotically with nature rather than detached from it.

The traditional scientific worldview puts man firmly in the middle (often separate and deemed superior) to other life forms, and possibly leading to a blinkered view of *what is*. The Universe is unfolding as it should; naturally – according to its laws, some of which science knows and has labelled, others maybe just glimpsed, and some (or perhaps many) currently unknown to the scientific community. The parallel paths of science and spirituality are becoming more convergent, with overlaps and cross-overs happening regularly, perhaps shedding light upon, and connecting us more to, The Great Mystery.

The Sun and Moon

The Sun and Moon have been honoured and worshipped throughout human history, associated with gods and goddesses, surrounded by story and legend, and their motion used to divine prophecy. These two celestial bodies, of course, significantly affect life on our planet. The Sun bathes the Earth with its spectrum of illuminating, warming and electromagnetic rays; the energy that drives all life on earth, and an energy we can harness through solar panels as electricity to power our modern lives. The Sun's path across the sky is an aid for navigation and marks the passing of the day. And at dawn and dusk, we can witness the mesmerising colour show as the sun seemingly morphs between golden yellow, orange and red, as the shorter wavelength colours of blue and violet are scattered by the increased amount of atmosphere the rays have to pass through.

The Moon, changing its face each night as it waxes and wanes, pulling on the tides and all water on the planet, marking cycles of plant growth and female fertility, reflecting down a soft silvery light as a beacon in the darkness of night and the cosmic coincidence that it is exactly the right size for a total eclipse[29], all make it no surprise that, as the Sun's night-time twin, the Moon is also revered.

Science may tell us the Sun and Moon's composition, age, motion within the solar system and path across the sky, but the influence of these heavenly bodies remains prevalent upon our psyches, as both are also powerful when used in spiritual practices. Ancient civilizations constructed circles and temples aligned to the Sun, such as Stonehenge and the Great Pyramid at Giza, and many current annual festivals, celebrations or ceremonies happen on or around the solar equinoxes and solstices.

The phases of the Moon chart the month and again have always guided the timing of particular spiritual practices. The new moon is a moment for introspection and deciding upon a project or endeavour to embark upon. The waxing moon a time of action to move towards your desired results. The energy and light of the full moon harnessed in rituals and celebrations to savour your labours. And the waning moon signals a period of letting go of that which no longer serves, and finding inherent balance. Personally, I find the

---

[29] Although being four hundred times smaller than the Sun, the Moon is also about four hundred times closer to the Earth.

first and third quarter phases, when the moon is half in shadow and half in light, to be a perfect symbol of balance.

So get to know your solar and lunar calendars (there are many apps available for this), and maybe take a deeper look at the cycles of the year with their differing energies, known in the neo-pagan world as sabbats. The eight sabbats of the wheel of the year are:

Imbolc (1st-2nd Feb)   - New beginnings.
Ostara (19-22 Mar)   - Balance of day and night. Spring equinox.
Beltane (1st May)   - Growth and abundance.
Litha (19-23 Jun)   - Longest day. The Sun. Summer solstice.
Lammas (1st Aug)   - Midsummer.
Mabon (21-24 Sep)   - Harvest. Autumn equinox.
Samhain (Oct 31st)   - Halloween. Day of the dead.
Yule (starts 21 Dec)   - Shortest day. The Moon. Winter. Christmas.

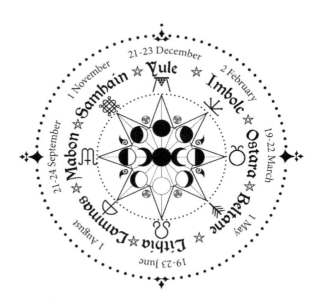

Sun gazing
Note: Safety warning

Never look directly at the Sun. You will do permanent damage to your eyesight.

With eyes closed, look in the direction of the Sun and *see* the light behind your eyes. Notice how it changes over time. It may begin as yellow but then turn to orange, red or maybe violet. Fill yourself with this colour, allowing it to seep into every corner of your body, to cleanse and energise. Try this at sunrise or sunset, noticing the often more peaceful environment at these times of day.

Moon wash

The reflected sunlight from the surface of the Moon is not bright enough to cause damage to your eyes, so looking directly at the Moon is quite safe. Ideally on or near a full moon, gaze gently at our natural satellite and breathe in the reflected silvery light, allowing it to move and shimmer throughout your body, flushing you with silver before flowing from your feet into the earth. Bathe in this moonlight, allowing it to wash over you completely.

If you have access to a lake or pond, try moon washing with the light directly from the Moon and its reflection in the water, doubling the potency.

The night sky

Who hasn't looked up at the night sky and been in awe? When doing so, we connect to our ancestors, who looked up just as we have and felt the same sense of insignificance and wonder. Sadly though, light pollution has taken away this opportunity from many people. A few years ago, during a stargazing tour in La Palma, Canary Islands, the guide shared with us her belief that most children born at that time would never see The Milky Way with their own eyes. So make the effort to go to a dark sky place and take in the night sky.

Astrology is not part of this book and is a decision for you on how much credence you give to it. However, it is known through science, specifically astronomy, that we share this solar system with other planets, none of which currently (it is believed) sustain life. The planets move across the heavens and are wonders to behold on a clear night with the piercing brightness of Venus or the red hue of Mars visible with the naked eye. With binoculars or a telescope (and a steadying tripod), it is possible to see the rings around Saturn as a small disc or the moons of Jupiter as dots of unblinking light adjacent to the planet. From an astronomical perspective, Jupiter is earth's protector, its gravity scooping up all the comets that would otherwise be bound for us. So maybe give a little thank you when you see it in the night sky.

The planets are part of the mythology of humanity, named after gods and goddesses, and inspiration for classical music, poetry and science fiction. Folklore has arisen around the planets, and astrology along with it, with each planet given a character or a set of traits, perhaps reflecting aspects of ourselves.

The Sun, Moon, planets and stars are natural wonders above us: guiding our way, providing light in the dark, inspiring dreams, fables and myths, and drawing us to look deeper into the Universe and strengthening our connection to something bigger.

The Unimaginable

Much is difficult for us to comprehend or even be aware of, especially if it is seemingly so detached from our daily lives. From the minutely small to the extremely large, from the invisible (to us) to the incomprehensibly big. But these things are worth thinking about, trying to comprehend and perhaps re-framing or scaling to aid understanding.

Our Universe exploded into being about 13.8 billion years ago, with the Earth forming some 4.5 billion years ago, the first microbial life about 3.5 billion years ago, complex life about 580 million years ago and the first human-like creatures (homo-habilis) around 3 million years ago. A single calendar year can represent this history of the Universe – a cosmic calendar starting with the Big Bang at midnight Jan 1st, to now, just before midnight Dec 31st. The Earth would have coalesced at the beginning of September, with the first life coming towards the end of that month. Complex life doesn't emerge until Dec 5th, with humans arriving at about 22:24 on Dec 31st. Homosapiens don't join the party until eight minutes to midnight Dec 31st, and the past five-hundred years of human history are covered by just one second, from 23:59:59 to midnight Dec 31st!

We are, however, linked to the entire history of life on our planet by the air we breathe, or, more accurately, by the 1% of our atmosphere that is the gas argon. Argon is an inert gas and does not combine readily with other elements, remaining chemically the same since the atmosphere first coalesced. These airborne argon atoms, breathed by prehistoric animals and ancient peoples, are now being inhaled by us, and will be breathed by those to come after us. We are connected across the millennia by argon, and similarly by the other inert gases, such as helium and neon. In fact, as matter is never destroyed, only transformed, we are all made up of material that has been recycled and re-purposed since its creation during the Big Bang, subsequently transmuted and redistributed by exploding supernovae.

Our bodies are in a constant battle, but are we aware of the self-healing that is going on? Fighting off infections and diseases, repairing broken bones or growing new cells? As previously mentioned (see *The North* section) our body's maintenance schedule replaces cells at varying rates, from a few days for the intestinal wall to seven to ten years for the whole skeleton. Then we have within our skull what has been referred to as the most complex structure in the known universe – our brain; which we still know very little about – not a surprise, with a conservatively estimated 500 trillion synapses firing away.

The irrational number, pi (π), is roughly 3.14 and is used in calculating the geometry of circles, cylinders and spheres. This approximation isn't enough for some people and, to date, has been calculated to over thirty trillion decimal places, although the use of this incredibly accurate number is debatable. According to *QI* (a UK TV programme) thirteen decimal places would be enough to target a laser to within one inch on the voyager spacecraft, currently twelve and a half billion miles away on its cosmic journey; forty decimal places would be sufficient to calculate the diameter of the entire observable universe to an accuracy of the width of one hydrogen atom!

Then there is our sun, emitting a vast amount of energy, a fraction of which hits the Earth as electromagnetic waves. We, as humans, only see about 1/80th of these EM waves – light and colour; the visible spectrum. The rest are invisible to our eyes and consist of gamma rays, x-rays and ultraviolet rays at the shorter wavelengths of light, infrared, microwaves and radio waves at the longer wavelengths.

Are there other energies hidden from us? A spiritual energy, a frequency of consciousness, an energy of the Divine?

The very, very large and extremely small are both difficult to imagine, but they become more understandable when scaled down or up. For example, let's take the world's population to be eight billion. The cube root of eight billion is two thousand. Eight billion could therefore be represented by a cube with dimensions 2000 x 2000 x 2000. If the cube comprised grains of sand, diameter 0.5mm (about 20/1000th inch), the cube's length would be 1m (just over 3 feet). A relatively small cube of sand to represent the planet's population and, hopefully, not too difficult to imagine.

Let's now look at representing the number of atoms in the human body using the same grain-of-sand scale. With approximately 7×10^{27} (a seven with twenty-seven zeros after it) atoms in our bodies, we arrive at a cube of sand with length a little under 1000km (around 600 miles – or the distance between London and Berlin). Slightly harder to imagine than a 1m cube, but still feasible.... just.

[Cube root of 7×10^{27} = 1,913,000,000. Using 0.5mm diameter sand grains gives a cube side length of 956,500,000mm = 956.5km or about 600 miles.]

Similarly, in a 500ml (about 16fl oz) water bottle, there are 17×10^{24} water molecules. So in one 5ml teaspoon there are 17×10^{22} molecules of H_2O. The cube of sand representing the molecules in a teaspoon would therefore be 27.5km (17 miles) long. A seventeen-mile-high cube of sand to represent the number of molecules in a single teaspoon of water. That's twice the height long-haul passenger planes fly!

[Cube root of 17x10^22 = 55,000,000. Using 0.5mm diameter sand grains gives a cube side length of 27,500,000mm = 27.5km or about 17 miles.]

If we look at the very big such as our Solar System and beyond, the figures are again mind-boggling and of little meaning to us. The distance to our nearest neighbour, the Moon, is 384,000 km (239,000 miles), while it is 150 million km (93 million miles) to the Sun. Unfortunately, to fit on the pages of books and magazines, we have been brought up with disproportionate pictures of the solar system with all the planets pushed together. Fortunately, more accurate representations are now available in videos on the internet. For an immersive experience, there are scale models of the solar system in Stockholm, Zagreb, Anstuther (Scotland) and Somerset (England). At these sites, the public can spatially get to grips with the sizes and distances of our corner of the galaxy, especially with the walkable installations.

The Somerset Space Walk uses the Bridgwater and Taunton canal towpath to display proportional representations of the Sun and the eight planets, plus Pluto[30], along the 22km (14 mile) path using a scale of 1:530,000,000. The Sun is represented by a 2.5m (8 ft) wide fourteen-ton concrete sphere located at Higher Maunsel lock, with the inner planets nearby, within 67m (220 ft). Pluto, a tiny (just under 5mm (1/6th in)) diameter sphere on a plinth, is an 11km (7 mile) walk away, with the other outer planets en route along the towpath. On this scale, the nearest star to our Solar System, Proxima Centauri, would be a red ball 38cm (15 in) in diameter but impossible to site, as it would need to be 76,000 km (47,000 miles) away; roughly twice the circumference of the Earth!

---

[30] The Somerset Space Walk was constructed before Pluto was reclassified as a dwarf planet.

Are we alone in the Universe?

It was such a cosmic coincidence that life began on earth that it is quite possible we are alone in the Universe. There is likely to be bacteria or primitive organic matter on other worlds, if water is present, but any form of complex and intelligent life may be limited to our planet.

The rare earth hypothesis states that Earth is the only place where life has begun, due to the unique circumstances that have played out. These include the Earth's distance from the Sun being within the *goldilocks* zone (where water can exist as a liquid), the protection from asteroid impact provided by Jupiter's immense gravity and the atmosphere's ability to regulate temperature and reflect into space dangerous cosmic rays. Additionally, the magnetic field generated by the rotation of the iron core also deflects harmful radiation. The moon too plays its part, as it is tidally locked to the Earth, reducing wobble and keeping the Earth's tilt angle steady. This tilt angle has given us the seasons and a stable enough environment for life to begin and, ultimately, thrive. In fact, it is believed the moon was responsible for generating the tilt angle in the first place, when it impacted the Earth early in the formation of the Solar System, knocking our planet off its axis.

If we are alone, that makes us a miracle – so we should feel very special indeed. Of course, we take life for granted and go about our daily lives oblivious to the astounding coincidences and occurrences that led to us being here. Are there other miracles are out there that may have passed many of us by? Are spirit encounters, spiritual or shamanic healings or magical synchronicities wondrous miracles that should be accepted as reality, however improbable they may seem? Instead of impossible, they suddenly become possible.

Connecting with the unknown and unknowable

Contemplating the unknowable is akin to the Japanese koan, "what is the sound of one hand clapping?" The immediate answer seems impossible or out of reach. But by pondering the question and contemplating the unknowable, you are putting yourself in the space of somebody open to learning.

Being receptive to learning is crucial in acquiring knowledge. As any teacher knows, the student ready and willing to learn will be a joy to have in the class. The student that is not interested (for whatever reason) will not be engaged, be easily distracted, become bored and even be disruptive, affecting all others in the class.

So, how do you put yourself in a state of openness, ready to contemplate the unknowable? The most obvious way is by meditating. Meditation is an excellent way to take steps towards connecting to whatever is inside and outside of yourself. To link to that which is known and to that which is unknown, or even unknowable, by clearing the mind and simply being.

As an exercise, while in meditation, allow yourself to connect with the Universe; to go out into the cosmos or up to heaven and be with Great Spirit, God, Goddess or that which is beyond, whatever you call *it*. If *it* is beyond your understanding or comprehension, or outside of your comfort zone, then just accept this as being so, but also accept that maybe *it* can hear you or *it* can be with you. You don't have to call *it* God, spirit or anything you are uncomfortable with, but you have to call *it* something. I suggest calling *it* the Universe and going from there. As you are part of this universe, maybe also accept that *it* may be part of you and not necessarily a separate entity. Visualise this force or energy, this deity or being. Feel connected to it. Commune with it.

Another method of connecting with the unseen is to observe the effects of the known invisible-to-human forces. Throwing a ball in the air and watching it come back down shows us the effect of gravity, the warmth of the Sun is evidence of the infrared rays emitted, while sunburn results from overexposure to the Sun's potent ultraviolet rays. Fridge magnets and a directional compass demonstrate the effects of magnetism. These energies and forces are unseen, but measurable with the correct scientific equipment. The question to contemplate, of course, is whether there are unseen energies and forces that remain hidden from science.

Heaven and Earth flow

This exercise is similar to some of the previous breath-flow practices but with a more physical approach, using movement to create an energy flow. Begin by standing and grounding yourself, imagining roots coming from your feet into the earth. Squat down, sweeping your hands across your legs in a gathering-earth-energy motion, before slowly standing, *pulling* this energy up with your hands, through the roots and your feet into your body. As your hands reach your chest, turn them over so you can continue the motion, now *pushing* the energy through the upper body, into your head and out of your crown and fingertips, extending your arms above you. Reverse the movement, *pulling* energy from the Universe into the top of your head, through your body, turning your hands over halfway and *pushing* it through the lower body, out of your feet and roots, sending the energy deep into the earth.

Imagine earthy brown energy, red molten lava, crystal clear water or a purifying colour being pulled up from the earth and flowing through your body, before being pushed out of the top of your head and outstretched arms heavenward. Whatever substance or colour feels right to you is fine. Conversely, visualise sunlight (gold), moonlight (silver), a mix of both (platinum) or maybe a white or indigo spiritual light when pulling energy down from above, letting it flow through your body into the ground. Breathe in when pulling in, from above or below, and breathe out when pushing out, up or down. Ensure the movements flow and find a rhythm.

Vary the visualisation and note any different effects. Swap between pulling up red magma, green grass or blue ocean water, and pulling down twinkling starlight, a colourful rainbow or a divine violet.

Connect with what is above

Feel the connections in nature that are above or that move upwards; trees growing, reaching for the light; an eagle soaring and swooping; flames, sparks and smoke darting up from a fire, drifting in the air. Lose yourself in cloud formations. Dream upon the vapour trails of planes as they pass overhead, imagining a far-flung exotic destination. Watch sunrises and sunsets and be in awe. Notice how the wildlife around you behaves at this time of the day. Lay on the ground under a stand of trees and gaze up along their trunks skyward. Climb up high, on a hill or mountain, and take in the view.

Always take in the view.

Communication

The use of language to communicate (the English language in this book's case) has its limitations and can be open to misinterpretation. As we probably all know (and have been guilty of), any form of texting, social media posting or emailing can easily be misunderstood or *taken the wrong way* by the reader. Shortened sentences, bullet points or headlines can fail to convey the intended meaning. Additionally, some words are far more loaded and open to various interpretations depending on a person's beliefs or viewpoint. For example, words such as love, god, goddess, spiritual, religion, power and energy have dictionary definitions, but their use in conveying a specific meaning varies greatly. Then there are cultural and translational differences between the languages of countries, regions and provinces, even between towns in the same area. The same words can have various meanings or mean slightly different things, especially when translated from one language to another. There is also the issue of comprehension and the use of vocabulary that the recipient may not fully understand. The written and spoken word alone are not enough for true communication.

Communication begins at an early age, even before birth, in the womb. Talking to baby, playing music and creating a good atmosphere can all affect the unborn child. The emotional and psychological state of the mother also has a profound impact on the developing baby. In the UK Channel 4 TV programme *Grayson Perry: Rites of Passage*, Dr Cyriac, consultant paediatrician at Broomfield hospital, Essex, UK, noted:

> *"If a mother is distraught... if I can reassure her and she leaves with a smiley face, I know the child will be ok, as it is the vibrations of the mother which is actually the healing for the child... Happy mother equals a happy child."*

The child feels and takes on emotions and energy from their mother, as I am sure any mother would attest to. From the father too, be it his voice, emotional tone or maybe his energy when nearby. Maybe also from others if they are regularly in close contact with the mother during the pregnancy. As mentioned in *The trauma of being born* chapter in *The South* section, issues causing trauma can be imparted to the unborn baby before it has had a chance to take its first breath – imparted non-verbally, chemically and energetically.

The non-verbal component of communication is vital to comprehension, as illustrated if we have ever tried to make ourselves understood in a foreign non-English speaking country by using tones, expressions and often exaggerated gesticulations. This non-verbal component is also significant when we talk to others or watch interviews where the words spoken do not seem to match the speaker's behaviour or bodily cues. Such conflicting actions can leave us unconvinced by what was said, possibly even giving us the impression that the other person does not believe what they are saying, is acting or lying. Non-verbal communication experts can be highly valuable in interview scenarios or as political correspondents to the media.

Taking this a step further, underlying this non-verbal communication is the intention of the communicator to impart a meaning, both subconsciously when being genuine, or consciously when trying to persuade or mislead. The thought-form that drives this intention can be deemed the energy of the intention. In our conscious lives, we are constantly thinking and, therefore, creating these thought-forms, generally in our native language. If it is questionable how much is communicated through language – through words alone – then we must be cautious when listening to our internal monologue. Perhaps we should be more focused on the imagery our minds create as an accompaniment to our words rather than just the words on their own.

If we close our eyes (or soften our focus), we can visualise, imagine and create pictures internally. We know that a picture paints a thousand words and it is no different in our mind. The image, or images we conjure up, can capture and impart much more meaning than a string of sentences. They can trigger emotions and feelings surrounding the images or the scenario playing out in our mind. Typically, artists not only wish to create a beautiful or striking piece of art but, perhaps more crucially, they desire to impart specific emotions and sensations. The artist wants to stir up feelings and delve into emotions that are, by nature, complicated and difficult to describe verbally. As the American painter, Edward Hopper, said, "If I could say it in words, there would be no reason to paint."

Visualisations and self-help exercises (including many of those detailed in this book) are used to recreate scenarios and situations where we can manifest or tap into particular emotions and feelings, and embody them to some degree. This can help us express and release any harmful emotions safely and consciously rather than letting them overwhelm or hijack us in our daily lives. Moreover, visualisations of successful scenarios allow us to feel and rehearse – almost live through – desired outcomes. Such internal enactment can create new neurological pathways in our brain and a 'field of intentional energy' within our body, familiarising us with this vibration of achievement. This ability to imagine ourselves winning is a powerful tool used by many professionals, from athletes to entrepreneurs, politicians to military leaders, and can be adapted to any life situation where we desire a self-administered boost.

Unwanted emotions and feelings, repeating negative monologues or thought-forms, can also be sidelined by going into silence through meditation, taking us beyond the chattering mind and allowing us to regain control. Meditation can take many forms, from the closed eyes and sitting quietly type, to the active meditations of walking, cleaning, playing an instrument, chanting, driving or listening to music. Any activity where we feel fully engaged, on auto-pilot or in the flow, is a form of meditation. We are trying to move away from our ego selves, open up to the flow of life and, in a sense, commune with something outside of ourselves.

Communication with people is one thing, but what about with the more-than-human world – with animals, plants or even the elements of earth, fire, water and air? All pet owners know that their animal understands them to some degree, albeit not a comprehension of the spoken words, but a mixture of the tone, gesture or positive reinforcement (through treats or affection) when a desired behaviour is displayed. If we encounter a wild animal, we are not looking to control its behaviour, but I am sure we would all like to communicate with it.

Dr Doolittle aside, how would we talk to the animals? Well, exactly as we would speak to another person. The animal does not understand the words spoken, but if we are genuine, the thought-form, the non-verbal communication and the intentional energy can be imparted. Pets and animals in captivity pick up on this. For example, horse owners and trainers know how responsive to emotions their animals can be, highlighted by their use in mental health therapy. Horses are particularly helpful with children (and some adults with learning difficulties) as they are naturally emotionally sensitive, having not built up the internal ego blocks of adults. Being with animals, especially pets that we can touch and hold, offers many benefits to our well-being, from the tactile contact of another living creature to the emotional boost of the animal's companionship and the often unconditional love given.

After training, pets or working animals may associate the sound of a word we say with a particular command, but they do not comprehend the word spoken. They have their own language. As do all animals and, for that matter, all organisms. Michael Prime, a guest on the BBC TV programme *Autumnwatch*, has developed an instrument to measure the faint bio-electrical signals produced by fungi that fluctuate depending on the state of the fungus. His equipment can convert these fungal communications into audible electronic noises, and has used the sounds (along with recordings of other plant life) in art installations, audio tracks and several CDs.

Trees also have their methods of communication, one of which (as previously mentioned in the *Mother Earth* section) is by connecting with other trees via their roots and the underground network of fungal mycelium strands. By using this *wood-wide-web* network, a tree can send help messages for required nutrients or signal a warning of an attack from pests, an unwanted bacterium or fungus, giving other trees time to raise their defences. The language of the trees, of course, is not English but chemical and electrical signals. However, underlying this communication is the desire to impart a meaning, in this case, 'I need phosphorous' or 'warning, harmful beetle infestation.' The tree is communicating with an energy of intention, which could be argued as showing a form of intelligence.

So if a tree can communicate, can we as humans commune with it? If we touch, hug or sit under a tree, and allow space for the tree's form of communication to merge with ours, then I believe such communication is possible. That is, to allow the tree's energy of intention to manifest within us through imagery, emotions and feelings. The tree has a basic level of understanding of our intention, generated through our thought-form and imparted energy, rather than comprehending any words spoken. In fact, I suggest this is the case for all plant and animal life and, to some degree, for the elements and inanimate objects. Botanists, horticulturists and many gardeners are well-versed in talking to their plants, while zoo keepers, horse whisperers and pet reiki practitioners all commune with the animals they care for.

Communication is also happening when we sit around a fire, swim in a river, stand on a cliff in the wind or put our hands in the earth as we tend the soil. This communication may seemingly be one-way and purely on an emotional level, but it is only the barrier of a rigid indoctrinated belief that two-way communication is impossible that stops us from attempting it. However, we can communicate with the more-than-human world, at some level, via intention, connection and energy. To do so, we must make an effort to tune in, open up all of our senses and create space for the communication to take place.

This has been a cornerstone of shamanic practice throughout history as, from a shamanic viewpoint, everything is alive, has its own spirit and energy, and is linked by the web of life. From the trees and plants to the rocks and mountains, from the raindrops to the oceans, from the wind to the stars, all is in a harmonious conversation of being. We can join in with that communication simply by conversing with nature – by talking, sensing or feeling and allowing our intention to come from the heart. If we are still, open and patient, then the conversation may be two-way, with a response coming in the form of a feeling, an image in our mind or even a real-time sign from nature, such as a sound, an object stumbled upon or an animal encounter.

As humans, we are drawn to natural objects. We enjoy touching, holding or simply looking at them. Wooden objects, rocks, crystals, shells, plants and flowers all have special places in our homes. If there is a natural object that you like to hold or feel connected to in some way, then maybe it is trying to communicate with you. Perhaps there is an energetic vibration emanating from the object that resonates with you, a message spoken without words. Try sitting in meditation or journeying while holding the object.

Often these objects can be seen as talismans, which may seem to take on magical properties over time, especially if they have been used effectively in healing work on ourselves or with others.

More accepted as having potent properties are the chemically active compounds found in nature, used in their raw form by herbalists, healers and lay folk (with a little knowledge) and synthesised by chemists into modern medicines.

So with talismans, objects from nature and natural remedies in mind, clearly, there is some truth in the stories of the medicine cabinets of witches and wizards being full of interesting natural objects. Please note, I am entirely against the hunting, farming or exploitation of animals for their body parts, as often associated with traditional Chinese medicine.

Our body also communicates. Our physiological systems are interconnected and communicate via the nervous and endocrine systems. These systems feed back information on internal health (in the form of pains, palpitations or sensations), generate certain feelings and emotions using hormones and inform us of the external world, via our senses. This direct communication is coupled with more sublime forms, such as our intuition, the vibrations we pick up from other people or places and the metaphors of our dreams; all ways in which something outside of our immediate consciousness is trying to get our attention.

Nature expresses herself, for want of a better word, naturally. We, as humans, have evolved a language of words to try and express ourselves, but we often fall short when it comes to conveying the totality of what we want to say. We are limited by language and our vocabulary. Writers, poets and playwrights have strived to rectify this when describing the human condition. As do other creative souls: the artist with an evocative painting, ethereal drawing or sublime sculpture, the chef that stirs something deep inside with the presentation, smell and taste of their exquisite food or the musician tugging at our heartstrings.

Perhaps the purest form of musical expression is classical music. Without lyrics to misinterpret, the listener can be taken away solely by the sounds of the instruments and the emotions evoked by the composition. At a more fundamental level, sound repetition – chanting, mantra reciting, drum beating or rattle shaking – can occupy the ego mind and create space for communication to occur with something outside ourselves. We just have to be open to it.

The Centre - Sovereignty, balance and authenticity

*"We are all masters of our own destiny. We can so easily
make the same mistakes over and over. We can so easily
flee from everything that we desire and which life so
generously places before us.
Alternatively, we can surrender ourselves to Divine
Providence, take God's hand, and fight for our dreams,
believing that they always arrive at the right moment."*
Paul Cohelo, Brida.

Ultimately, life is up to you. Whatever your background, experiences, setbacks and traumas, or colour of skin, gender or nationality, your life is your responsibility, nobody else's. It is up to you what you make of it. Allowing yourself to be dictated to by another (be it a person, company, government or culture), following the crowd blindly or blaming circumstances, parents, society, God or any other deity about the state of your life will not help in the long run. Do you have a relationship with life, with the more-than-human world outside of *you*, spiritual or otherwise? Are you in control of this, or is it something inherited or you feel obliged to conform to?

Working on yourself will highlight areas that may need improving or where the negative influences can be lessened, showing where you can change your thoughts, behaviours and habits. You can find deeper meaning, more value in all things, see beyond the day-to-day and accept difference in yourself and others.

To sit at the centre of all that is inside and outside of you requires the ability to be a witness to your life, not just a participant. To be an observer. To discern, understand and incorporate lessons. To change, accept or let go of that which does not serve you. To encourage self-confidence, even if faced with the unknown. To ask for help. And to listen for, and act upon, the answer. In doing all this you, realise that you are at the centre. You are in charge. You have to take responsibility. This is sovereignty. King or queen (or both) of all you have influence over.

The law of attraction

If you have read spiritual books, gone to workshops or listened to spiritual advice, then the law of attraction is always to be found. I'm not sure who made it law, and I don't doubt it can be broken, but the general premise behind it has some validity, even if science and, in particular, the science of quantum, is only now beginning to understand why. This attraction stems from the idea that our thoughts create our reality. The energy behind our thoughts can be creative in its intention, drawing towards us similarly vibrating energy forms and, perhaps, also providing an insight into the fundamentals of consciousness. This energy is currently beyond scientific measure, but will surely be observed and clarified one day.

As this law is indiscriminate, negative and positive thoughts are treated the same. Therefore, you need to make a conscious effort to drop negative thinking and stay focussed on the positives. Focus on what you DO want, not what you don't want. Continually worrying about what you don't want to happen only draws it closer to you. Notice when negative thoughts come up. Catch them, block them or re-frame them into a positive. In *The Power Within You Now!* Sue Stone says:

> *"When a thought (vibration) is repeated, the brain attaches emotion to it, this is stored in the subconscious*

and acted upon behind the scenes. Good or bad, positive or negative, true or false, the subconscious does not differentiate. Where conscious thoughts are leading, the subconscious will follow."

So start by putting yourself in an open and receptive state, ideally in a state of love. Visualise love in any way you choose – a partner, a child, a love of life, a love of nature, a love of yourself. Breathe deeply and let the expression of love expand from your heart throughout your body and travel out as far and wide and as all-embracing as you wish. Next, focus on what you want to attract and draw into your life. Visualise yourself already having it. Bring it alive, allowing the experience to flow through you to all parts of your body. Finally, rest in gratitude, in appreciation of what you wish to receive, knowing it is coming to you.

Visualise and embody the life you want as though it is already here. Working with affirmations, visualisations and your vision board can help with this. Please note, positive thinking alone, without embracing the feelings of success or achieving your desires, is likely to fail and could leave you disappointed and disillusioned. As will be looked at later, the ancient philosophers of the stoic and similar schools realised that life's highs (and lows) should be seen as outside judgements and, to some degree, psychological imposters. Like many of the Eastern religions, the Stoics also suggest cultivating detachment to help lead a calmer, more peaceful and happier life.

Archetypes and characteristics

We all have specific characteristics. Some inherited, others developed throughout our lives. Psychologists have labelled these generalised characteristics and use them to differentiate and distinguish people, perhaps showing where strengths or weaknesses lie. Such categorising includes the Warrior, Settler or Nomad – described by hypnotherapist Terrence Watts[31] – to profile our subconscious drivers; the sixteen personality types – outlined in the Myers-Briggs test – used by recruitment consultants to streamline job candidates; and the roles people play in teams – such as those described by Belbin – to help corporations develop the optimal team structures. All are based on the individual's personality and characteristics, and how they interact with others and the world.

As an experiment during my studies at university, I devised a questionnaire, completed by my classmates, that would broadly show which Belbin team role they would fall into. The nine roles Belbin proposed are Resource Investigator, Teamworker and Co-ordinator (the Social roles); Plant, Monitor Evaluator and Specialist (the Thinking roles); and Shaper, Implementer and Completer Finisher (the Action or Task roles). Based on these characteristics, I split the class into several smaller groups for a simple teamwork exercise. I purposely comprised each team with people with the same or similar characteristics, e.g., a group containing only the social roles or another only thinking roles. However, I formed one team that consisted of each Belbin role. This group outperformed the others and completed the task first – and with the least amount of team friction.

The results from my simple university experiment, and any similar method of categorising people, demonstrate how people or groups can be chosen, worked with or manipulated based on their character. They can also highlight where certain traits may be lacking or point to the aspects of an individual's personality that should be worked upon if they wish to grow.

---

[31] Terrence Watts, *Warriors, Settlers and Nomads*, 2000, Crown House Publishing.

Perhaps a more soulful and nature-connected viewpoint on archetypes is that described by Bill Plotkin in his book *Wild Mind* and termed the *four facets of wholeness*[32]:

- *Nurturing Generative Adult*: Compassionate, courageous, competent, knowledgeable and exhibits heart-centred thinking; i.e., independent, critical, creative, moral. A benevolent king or queen, spiritual or peaceful warrior, mature and caring mother or father.

- *Innocent/Sage*: Able to see the bigger picture, innocent, wise, clear-minded, light-hearted, wily, extroverted and exhibits full-presence sensing; i.e., alive to the five senses. Represented by the sacred fool or trickster, priest, priestess, guide to spirit.

- *Wild Indigenous One*: Emotive, sensuous, instinctive, playful, erotic-sexual, fully at home in the human body and the more-than-human world. Exhibits full-body feeling; i.e., gut feeling, body and organ awareness, hunches, vibes, sexual passion, in touch with emotions. Represented by Pan, Artemis/Diana, the Green Man.

- *Muse/Inner Beloved*: Imaginative, erotic-romantic, idealistic, visionary, adventurous, darkness-savouring, introverted and exhibits deep imagination; i.e., images, dreams and visions. Represented by magician, wanderer, hermit, psychopomp, anima/animus, guide to soul.

These archetypes are at play when we are pulled by a calling to discover more about life and our part to play within it. Bill calls this *the descent to the Soul*[33] (a Western and contemporary take on adult initiation), and is similar to the journey Carl Jung took that eventually led to the field of depth psychology.

[32] Bill Plotkin, *Wild Mind: A Field Guide to the Human Psyche*, 2013, New World Library.
[33] Bill Plotkin, *The Journey of Soul Initiation: A Field Guide for Visionaries, Revolutionaries, and Evolutionaries*, 2021, New World LIbrary.

Acceptance

We are all different, but we are connected by our shared humanity. Therefore at the root of balance, harmony, integration, diversity, community and society is acceptance. Acceptance of race, religion, culture, sexual orientation, politics, education and personality. These categories, however, are also the obvious areas of difference, most notably when we see or hear something we are unfamiliar with, don't like or disagree with.

Differences crop up in less obvious ways too. Take smell, for example, probably the most evocative of the senses and often forgotten when it comes to acceptance. Like it or not, we all have our own odour – the way we smell to others – with many of us using fragrances, in the form of perfume, aftershave or deodorant, to change or mask our aroma. Pheromones are also at play here and can be decisive when meeting a potential partner. Being attracted to their smell is a positive and often arousing sign. Being repulsed by their scent indicates that you may not be compatible as mates or life-long partners.

Similarly, we all have our own sound. Our accent. The sound when we speak, based on dialect, tone and timbre, loudness and rhythm, and fundamentally, on the language of our region or country. It forms part of our cultural identity. We accept other people's accents (even if we may not like them), but we don't dismiss them as people because of how they speak. The vocal taunts or accent mimicry between rival countries, for example, Australia, England and USA, are accepted as sarcasm and banter, often around sporting competitions. This can sometimes be viewed as veiled racism but is, in my experience, just part of the gamesmanship between competitive egos.

Additionally, not liking a particular accent or how somebody speaks is not necessarily racist. As with smell, it is human nature. Not liking how someone sounds is the same as not liking their aroma, how they dress or anything else about them. It is a natural, almost primal, reaction to the unfamiliar – not racist. Imagine a pupil starting mid-term at a new school. This pupil comes from another part of the country and has a strong regional accent. There is a chance he will be made fun of for his accent by some of the other students, being taunted or having his words repeated back to him in an exaggerated comical way. On the other hand, some classmates may find his voice interesting, even attractive, and is a characteristic that separates him from the rest, making him stand out from the crowd.

As creatures of habit, we are comfortable with the familiar; our routines, the people we work and share our life with. Our community. Change or the unfamiliar – new places, new people, new ideas – can be challenging and initially, difficult to accept. Often though, with time, we become familiar with the new and can accept the differences, even come to embrace them. Moving to a new home with different neighbours and starting a new school or job takes time to *settle* into. If the move is to a different country, the challenges may be greater but not insurmountable, as proven by the number of people who emigrate.

A simpler example of acceptance is trying a new hot drink or removing sugar from tea or coffee. Initially, you may not like it and it may even disgust you, but over time your taste buds adjust and you come to accept and enjoy the new drink.

Then there is the more controversial category of people's appearance – their facial features, body shape and size, skin colour, clothing, mannerisms and how they carry themselves. Again, we are attracted to certain traits and characteristics, indifferent or not attracted to others. In the mating game, we are often attracted to those that look similar to us. To those we are familiar with or conform to the archetype we are usually attracted to – giving us the phrase, "He/she is not my type". Of course, this is not always the case as beauty is never only skin deep.

Taking this one step further, we also have our own energy. You may link this to character and therefore say our nature dictates the energy we put out into the world. Some people captivate a room when they walk into it; others seemingly suck the atmosphere out. These are extremes and the vast majority lie somewhere in the middle, in the hump of the statistical bell-shaped *normal* curve.

So, it is easy to understand and accept that we don't like the same things, prefer certain smells over others, and have a particular palette regarding taste and what pleases the ear. The same can be said of physical appearance, skin colour, size or any other physical attribute. Again, this is not racist, but behaving naturally. Racism, along with other -isms (i.e., sex, size, age), excludes or chastises, penalises and brings attention to differences, for reasons of coercion, exploitation, abuse or entertainment. There is a distinction. We are all different and have different tastes and preferences, but we can treat everyone with respect, accepting each other, differences and all. The mind is powerful and can overcome the senses and our instinctual resistance with some effort, allowing us to see beyond the animalistic impulses of our mammalian brain and feel love for any and all people, and any and all animals for that matter. Where in your life do you struggle with acceptance of differences and others? Where, perhaps, are you being quick to judge?

The Doorway

Be standing to do this exercise, with enough space to step forward, turn around and step back. Close your eyes or wear a blindfold to go into darkness. Begin by imagining an ornate door set into a beautiful doorway in front of you, with a key on a hook off to one side. Take the key and unlock the door. Turn the handle and open the door away from you, revealing a beautiful world beyond. Step through the doorway into this imaginary domain, both in your mind and in the place you are physically standing in the ordinary world. As you cross the threshold, sense that you are leaving behind all of your troubles and issues in the everyday world, even if only briefly, and are stepping into a magical world of possibility, new opportunity and a place of miracles. Actively feel the old life left as something you have stepped away from. Feel your problems, worries or concerns all dissipate. They mean nothing in this brave new world you have stepped into.

Explore the landscape through this doorway. What does it look and feel like? Who or what exists here? Converse with this world. Talk with any beings or creatures you meet. Is there a stone circle here? If not, visualise one. Step into it and continue the conversation and journey in this realm. This is a world of creation. What does your heart, your soul, want to create? How can you make manifest your dreams and desires? Take time to explore this magical place and become familiar with it. [Feel free to sit down in the ordinary world if you feel you have been standing for too long, but remember to stand up again when ending the visualisation.]

When you have finished, return to the doorway and face it, looking back at your old life. It is there waiting for you if you want it, just as you left it a moment ago. However, to the right is another doorway, also leading back to the ordinary world, but this time it is to a new life; a new start, without the attachments of the previous life. Make your choice and walk through. Again as you take the step across the threshold in your visualisation, do so physically in the ordinary world. The door will automatically gently close behind you, but know you are welcome to return to this place and explore it whenever you wish.

Bring yourself back into the ordinary world, removing any blindfold and opening your eyes.

Lighthouse keeper exercise

This exercise is to put yourself at the centre of the storm, at the heart of the tempest, but able to weather it, knowing you are safe and being looked after. Visualise yourself as a lighthouse keeper on a rocky outcrop in the ocean; open to the elements, but protected. Your beacon shines brightly, warning of rocks and danger to seafarers. Allow a storm to rage as you watch safely from your lighthouse – almost in the elements but safe from harm. Feel the power but not the fear. Sense the sturdiness of the structure you are standing in, its capability to withstand the forces of nature thrown at it. Feel it rooted to the rock. Unmoving, unbending, unyielding. Feel these traits within yourself. Feel strong, powerful, resilient and grounded, whatever is happening in your life or the world around you.

Note: Safety Warning. This exercise can be especially potent during an actual storm, and can be carried out as you shelter in a building or somewhere safe outside, being mindful of a change in temperature, strong winds, falling branches or lightning.

Anchors and power places

What are your anchors? Those things that talk directly to your soul, enriching you beyond words, and can bring you back to a feeling of connection, to feeling yourself or maybe even provide a clue towards your purpose and place in this world? What do you turn to in a time of need or when you want to be uplifted and re-energised? And to what places do you go? Where do you feel at home, at peace, connected, inspired, feel yourself or comfortable being lost in the moment? Some examples of anchors are making, lighting and gazing at a real fire; the smell of smoke from a wood fire; holding a treasured talisman; spending time in nature; painting; working with wood; beating a drum; playing music; meditating; baking; the smell of the forest; exercise; breathing sea air; playing with your children (or grandchildren); a hot water bottle on your belly; knitting; chanting or singing; taking photographs; holding objects from your altar; being with your partner.

Anything can be an anchor for you, maybe having its root in your childhood, like a love of fishing, stroking a pet or standing out in the rain under an umbrella.

Similarly, power places can be anywhere; the beach; a particular bench in the park; your garden; under a tree; on a cliff top; at your football team's ground; a specific café or museum; standing in the wind or rain; your bedroom; on top of a mountain. You may have many and be drawn to each for a different reason.

Do you have a sit spot? A place in nature that you are drawn to and can come back to throughout the year, noticing the changing of the seasons. It is a place where you can sit quietly and connect with the nature around you, become familiar with any plants, trees or animals, along with the geology and geography of the area.

Conversely, the more time you spend here, the more the local flora and fauna become familiar with you and your energy. Try conversing with nature when in your sit spot, asking your most profound questions.

List out your anchors and power places, noticing any crossover or themes. Which have been with you throughout life? Which are relatively new? Are there ones you are drawn to but never explored?

Route home

This is a simple yet often illuminating exercise. Write down the people connections that have led you to where you are today. By this, I mean the people you have met, by introduction or because of another, that have brought you to where you are now. Include relatives, friends, teachers, colleagues or any other people key to your life chain. Start from now and take the linkage back to your parents and the place of your birth.

For example, let's say you met your romantic partner at your company's annual conference; you joined the company due to an introduction from an ex-colleague; met your ex-colleague on a meditation course; went to this course after a friend recommended it; knew your friend since school; went to the school you did because your parents moved to the area when you were an infant; your parents decided to move to be closer to your father's workplace; your place of birth was the house your mother inherited from your late grandmother. Would you have met your partner if there had been a break in this chain?

Take a moment to give thanks to each one of the people on your route home.

Balance

As human beings, we believe we can handle the pace of change we see on our planet, as we can use our brains to be flexible and adapt. Nature takes longer. The natural world's *brain* runs to a slower beat. Finding balance between the living organisms in an ecosystem takes many years and recovery from changes to that system is a long process. But restoring the balance is inevitable. Nature is programmed that way. To find balance.

This is also true for humanity. Deep down, our natural instinct is to find balance. Unfortunately, our minds and egos have somewhat taken over, and outside influences often pull us away from equilibrium. Influences from our culture, upbringing and the media all pull at us, requesting we behave in a particular way and conform to specific ideals. We feel coerced into buying things we don't need, expected to live and work at a seemingly increasing pace, and pressured to look a certain way to fit in. This constant bombardment and strain on our psyches does not lend itself to balance.

Therefore, we must take responsibility and move out of this daily drama of life, slow down a little and find our natural way of being – our personal rhythm and balance. Meditation and other spiritual pursuits lend themselves to this, even if only practised for a few minutes daily. Touching base with our internal selves, recognising where we may be out of balance and taking steps to rectify this, are often enough to keep us aligned and connected with our inner peace. The routine chores, everyday struggles and unexpected life issues will always be there to challenge us, especially in Western society, as will fears around safety, health, relationships and financial security. Allowing ourselves a brief moment of calm will act as an oasis of balance in what can be a fraught daily life.

Globally, being in balance has always been recognised as being worthwhile. In the three-thousand-year-old Indian holistic healing system of Ayurveda, balancing your doshas (the three bio-energy centres of vata, pitta and kapha) is important to physical and digestive health. Yoga too, incorporates finding balance by being in (and moving into and out of) specific postures called asanas. The philosophy includes yogic breathing techniques (known as pranayama – 'controlling life energy with the breath' in sanskrit), that can also help find balance, calm nerves, be useful in meditation, transmute negativity and help heal the body.

Tai-chi, qi-gong or practices based around flowing movements, again requiring physical balance, can lead to mental calmness. Staying in the East, the Chinese philosophy of yin and yang shows how balance is needed, often between two conflicting parts of the psyche, to create the whole. In the Western world, psychologists have embraced this principle to help clients find a balance between mental archetypes.

Being in balance is not about being in the middle or normal, it is knowing when you are being too much of one thing and not enough of its opposite. For example, when cultivating a balance with nature, you don't have to 'up sticks' and live sustainably in the forest. Maybe spending more time walking in a natural setting, away from urban life and its trappings, will be enough to swing the scales and provide moments of inner peace and harmony with your surroundings.

Emotional Freedom Technique (EFT)

Tapping on the body has been suggested a few times in this book and is worthy of further investigation if you have found it helpful.

According to EFT proponents, tapping on specific areas (most commonly acupuncture points) has a calming and therapeutic effect, helping with disorders, imbalances and such ailments as headaches, pains or anxiety. I have found tapping useful during a practice or ceremony to aid in clearing blocks or triggering an emotional release. Particular points to tap are the throat, left upper chest, belly area or karate chop point on the hands.

Talismans

Talismans are objects that are sacred or special to you. Ones you regularly keep in a pocket, on a key chain or are worn as jewellery. They could be objects from nature, a conker, a stone, a shell, a crystal, a piece of wood or man-made items such as a badge, ring, necklace, small toy or ornament. Ideally, keep them on your altar when they are not with you and decide after any daily meditation, affirmation or prayers which you wish to work with through the day. These are reminders of your connection to that outside of your conscious self, and I suggest only carrying or wearing one or two items each day, thus focusing the energy. Remember though, lucky talismans are only fortuitous because of the creative energy associated with them.

Beautiful objects, on the other hand, are inherently powerful because of their innate beauty to us. They do not have to be expensive, mystical or exotic. An acorn in its cup, a pressed flower or a small trinket can all have profound meaning. For many years I have used conkers, as I like how they feel in my hand and the direct connection with nature they provide. A conker can be found in most of my coat and jacket pockets, allowing me to easily tap into this connection to nature and something bigger as I hold it, even if on a train or walking the city streets.

The phrase "touch wood", uttered after a statement of purpose and hoping for good fortune, is usually accompanied by tapping something wooden – comically your head if there is no wood nearby. This phrase has only come into modern parlance because of the importance of trees throughout our history and the powerful and almost magical properties wood exhibits. So why shouldn't touching wood or being near it impart some of that magic? This is a common belief or assumption; being next to something (or someone) powerful or deemed lucky enhances us through association and proximity.

This leads nicely to the idea of energetic fields and the auras that all life emanates.

Energetic fields, auras and protection

There is a long list of detectable particles bombarding us continually day and night, many of which we are blissfully unaware of. From the cosmic microwave background radiation, generated at the dawn of time during the Big Bang, to the global magnetic field caused by the movement of Earth's molten iron core. But perhaps most significant is the radiation from our star. The Sun emits all wavelengths of the electromagnetic spectrum, from the visible to the invisible. Infrared, ultraviolet, microwave, x-rays, gamma rays, etc., all travel for eight minutes across the vacuum of space to interact with the atmosphere, land, seas and all life on this planet. These radiation waves are fundamental to the survival of most living organisms in one way or another.

The human body emits energy as heat, sound, electrical pulses and magnetic fields generated by our heart and nervous system. We also emit and detect chemical signals or pheromones, as many other animal species do, often to attract a mate. Animals use a variety of energy signatures as part of their daily lives, as a tool for food foraging, territory marking, nest locating or navigating migratory routes.

The planet is awash with signals, both naturally occurring and, ever more so nowadays, man-made. It is no surprise, then, that some people find themselves overloaded with sensory input, and may even feel physically unwell by the signals that surround and pass through them daily. Some have resorted to living off-grid, or more accurately, living far from the grid and the artificial signals generated, so they can live peacefully and, to their minds, healthily. Power grids and telecommunications masts are definitely a problem for some of the acutely sensitive in our society.

We know about being attracted to, indifferent about or repulsed by specific people – perhaps based on how they present themselves, their physical appearance, pheromones or odour, tone and accent, and their mannerisms and behaviour. These qualities, picked up upon through our senses, all build up our impression of them. But what about any other form of energy that people might emit? Is there a spiritual energy, a life-force energy or an energy of consciousness? Some sensitive people may well be able to tune into other frequencies, even to the energies of those that are deceased (e.g., psychics), just as others can tune in to the natural world (gardeners), to animals (vets), to their bodies (yogis) and to other people (empaths and (hopefully) psychologists).

According to mainstream science, seeing or measuring human spiritual energy is currently impossible. However, there are those people sensitive enough (or psychic enough) who say they can see the energy a person emits (their aura), and often link the colours sensed with spiritual insight. Popular within spiritual circles is a form of photography said to capture the aura around a person. It is based on the work of Russian scientist Semyon Kirlian, and was developed into an aura camera during the 1980s by American Guy Coggins. Kirlian photography may well produce colourful pictures, but there is, as yet, no evidence of its credibility.

There is, however, something at play here, as most people, whether they call themselves spiritual or not, can pick up on the energies of places and the emotions of others. For example, have you ever felt uneasy stepping into a particular bar, restaurant or shop due to the *atmosphere*, the architecture or maybe one or more of the people inside? Are you drawn to (or repelled by) certain places for no apparent reason? Have you ever been attracted to a particular person at a gathering, can feel their *good vibes*, or conversely, almost become physically sick by being too near certain people for an extended period? Many spiritual people find it challenging to be in crowds or travel on congested public transport, especially in confined spaces such as the London Underground, as they *pick up* on the abundance of energy (frequently deemed chaotic or negative) with no way to escape it.

If you are feeling out of sorts for no apparent reason, perhaps you are picking up on negative (or negatively perceived) energy from a person you are spending time with, from a place you frequent or even from the media. Spending too much time watching and reading the mainstream news or swiping through social media can significantly affect your energy levels. A constant stream of depressing and worrying reports can take its toll on the human psyche. Over prolonged periods this can influence the physical, often being noticed firstly in the gut and manifesting as digestive issues. Of course, spending too much time looking at electronic devices, whatever the reason, is not conducive to a healthy lifestyle.

As previously mentioned, living near power lines affects some people, as can living near other man-made objects, especially those not in keeping with the natural landscape such as grey, angular, concrete high-rise buildings; noisy, congested roads or motorways; busy airports; industrial and chemical plants; or over-crowded towns and cities. Are you living in or near a place that may be affecting you negatively?

We have looked briefly at individual power places earlier in this section, but there are also more general places where the energies are different, and perhaps more pronounced. These are usually places in nature that feel powerful; sometimes beautiful; sometimes foreboding. The geography and geology of the land, particularly the rock and water beneath, can have a notable effect on the energy felt in such places. Mapping these areas, either by feel or dowsing, has given us what are known as ley (or dragon) lines, forming part of a global grid of energetic connections. Sacred and culturally significant sites are often found on confluences of such ley lines, although little credence is given to this within the scientific community. And that is not a surprise, as no scientifically proven instrument is available to measure such lines of energy. Perhaps one day, there will be, and the property prices near such hotspots will rocket.

Suffice it to say that various energies surround and pass through us every day. Some absorbed, others radiated. It is clear that, with the right tools, they can all be measured, but, as has been said before, science will always lag behind what actually is. Until there are instruments sensitive enough to detect all the energies of the Universe, the existence of some of the more subtle ones will always be in doubt; but for those that feel them, they will forever be real. Therefore trust your instincts, and if you feel weird near an electrical pylon, a certain person or in a particular place, tune in to your senses and discern the issue. If this negative feeling is overly affecting you, it is best to clear your energetic field, the energy of your home and bring in some energetic protection.

You can clear your energy field by using some of the previously described clearing and *letting go* exercises, and purge your home by smudging or burning incense, beating a drum, chanting or singing while holding the intention to clear your space. Try to open a window or door at either end of your home and go into every room, flushing the unwanted or stagnant energies out and replacing them with fresh, uplifting and loving energy.

I have always struggled with the necessity of spiritual protection, as it is based on fear rather than love. Why should protection be needed? Shouldn't coming from a place of love be enough? Well, yes, I believe that is true. Still, I can guarantee that I have not always been able to get to that place of love, especially when I am out of sorts, feel ill, have my attention distracted by real-world issues or get all my buttons pressed by a confrontational encounter. Coming from a place of love then becomes highly challenging. So, asking for and generating protection is perhaps prudent. It was once explained to me as having your own bouncer at the door, just in case of trouble. An insurance policy, if you will.

Forms of protection vary, from calling in spirit, deities, holy people or totem animal allies; visualising protective auras, colours or bubbles around you; using an imagined shield or mirror to reflect back unwanted energy; or reciting prayers, spells or mantras for protection. Go with what feels right for you, but if protection and being protected are paramount to you, I suggest looking online for further information and techniques.

Personally, I believe that being in balance, in love with yourself and the world, and sharing that love are the best forms of protection.

Authenticity

Most of this book is concerned with looking at life from different perspectives, taking a deep look at yourself and moving to a more connected and spiritual life. Ultimately though, you have to be you. Life is not about being someone else. So, accepting your shadow self, your weaknesses and past mistakes, along with cultivating your strengths, natural abilities (your medicine) and looking to learn and grow where you can, are all part of being your authentic self.

Some authentic living tips from Lyn Christian, founder and coach at SoulSalt, are:

- Speak your opinions honestly in a healthy way.
- Make decisions that align with your values and beliefs.
- Pursue your passions.
- Listen to the inner voice guiding you forward.
- Allow yourself to be vulnerable and open-hearted.
- Set boundaries and walk away from toxic situations.[34]

Lyn goes on to say:

> "When you discover how to be your authentic self, you live in the flow. Creativity and abundance come to you effortlessly. Consistently living up to your core values

---

[34] Lyn Christian, *How to Be Your Authentic Self: 7 Powerful Strategies to Be True*, 22/03/21, SoulSalt.com.

leads to self-confidence. You trust yourself, and know that you can overcome obstacles when pursuing your goals. When you learn how to be real, you also create genuine relationships. You express yourself honestly, and therefore, attract like-minded people who support you, for who you really are."

Neil Pasricha, author of *You are Awesome*[35], adds:

"When you're authentic, you end up following your heart, and you put yourself in places and situations and in conversations that you love and that you enjoy. You meet people that you like talking to. You go to places you've dreamt about. And you end up following your heart and feeling very fulfilled."

A considered life

The human condition and how to live well have been at the centre of humanity's thinking for millennia. Perhaps the clearest guidelines came from the philosophies of the ancient Greeks, in particular, Socrates, Plato, Aristotle and the balanced and restrained approach to life as prescribed by the Stoics.

Stoicism still holds true even if you are on a path that includes spirituality or religion, although much philosophy shuns the need for any faith in a force or entity separate from the self. If you have doubts about some of the more esoteric or fuzzy areas of spirituality and religion, then the more rational approach offered by stoicism and similar philosophies may fill any gaps.

[35] Neil Pasricha, You are Awesome, 2019, Gallery Books.

Some pointers from the Stoics are:

- *Turn life's obstacles into opportunities.* Embrace life's challenges as a way to advance and improve. There are lessons to be learnt from the traumas, dramas and issues that come our way, however unwanted they may seem at the time. Review the examples from your *Life CV* in *The South* section.

- *Focus on what you can change, and don't worry about the things you can't.* Only your thoughts and actions are under your control; everything else is not. You always have control over how you respond to a situation or a problem. Waiting for spiritual intervention, the hand of God or any other helping input, is deferring to that which you cannot control. It may well happen, and you may be able to influence it, but I suggest it is prudent not to wait and take action yourself. You have to take the reins of your own life and, if at all possible, your death. (See *The West* section.) The Serenity prayer is stoic advice we are probably all familiar with:

  > *God, grant me the serenity to accept the*
  > *things I cannot change,*
  > *Courage to change the things I can,*
  > *And the wisdom to know the difference.*

- *It is not events that disturb people, it is their judgement about them.* When affected by a situation or an encounter, what is being reflected back to you? What are you seeing? And perhaps more importantly, what are you not seeing or understanding?

- *We suffer more in imagination than in reality.* Don't dwell in the mind.

- *Don't fear death. Use it to give your life value.* We all die eventually, so don't waste the precious time that you do have. Live immediately. *Carpe diem* – seize the day. Don't put off till tomorrow what you can do today. Take action.

- *Take time to review your day.* Practice having a daily reflection or a moment of peace for contemplation and meditation, and spend time in gratitude for what you have.

- *Maintain perspective and see the bigger picture.* Take the Eagle/Condor view. (See *The East* section.) Take a step back and realise that nothing is ever as important as it seems in the moment. Of course, bad things happen, so don't be surprised; be prepared for them.

- *You never stop learning.* Keep an open mind and allow yourself the freedom to learn and improve. Spiritually we are children and know so little. Don't be ashamed to ask for help. (See *The North* section.) As Plato said, *"The more I know, the more I realize I know nothing."*

- *Approach life with curiosity* and assume that everyone you meet may know something you don't.

- *Test and stretch yourself.* Associate with those that will improve you. Welcome those that you can improve. Share the love.

The poem *If*, by Rudyard Kipling (1865-1936) written in 1895, is an example of Victorian-era stoic wisdom and restraint, and was voted Britain's favourite poem in a 1995 BBC poll:

If you can keep your head when all about you
  Are losing theirs and blaming it on you,
If you can trust yourself when all men doubt you,
  But make allowance for their doubting too;

If you can wait and not be tired by waiting,
  Or being lied about, don't deal in lies,
Or being hated, don't give way to hating,
  And yet don't look too good, nor talk too wise.

If you can dream - and not make dreams your master;
  If you can think - and not make thoughts your aim;
If you can meet with Triumph and Disaster
  And treat those two impostors just the same;
If you can bear to hear the truth you've spoken
  Twisted by knaves to make a trap for fools,
Or watch the things you gave your life to, broken,
  And stoop and build 'em up with worn-out tools.

If you can make one heap of all your winnings
  And risk it on one turn of pitch-and-toss,
And lose, and start again at your beginnings
  And never breathe a word about your loss;
If you can force your heart and nerve and sinew
  To serve your turn long after they are gone,
And so hold on when there is nothing in you
  Except the Will which says to them: 'Hold on!'

If you can talk with crowds and keep your virtue,
  Or walk with Kings - nor lose the common touch,
If neither foes nor loving friends can hurt you,
  If all men count with you, but none too much;
If you can fill the unforgiving minute
  With sixty seconds' worth of distance run,
Yours is the Earth and everything that's in it,
  And - which is more - you'll be a Man, my son!

Love and fear

There are only two emotions at the root of all we do. We act out of love, or we act out of fear. Love is our natural state; but there is a place for some fear within our lives.

Rational fear helps keep us safe from predators, hypothermia, dehydration, being burnt, falling from a height or other potentially dangerous situations. It triggers our fight or flight response, boosting our energy levels to deal head-on with the issue or, alternatively, escape it, if that is deemed the best course of action. However, our encounters with rational fear are very much limited in the modern world, as rules, safety measures and cultural norms have restricted, reduced or even eliminated such threats.

Has this gone too far? Has the health and safety culture robbed us of feeling this rational fear and having adrenaline pumping through our veins, connecting us to the vibrancy and aliveness of the planet?

The search for this *chemical buzz* is reflected in the uptake of extreme sports and escapist action-packed video games, or the rise in popularity of horror movies and scary TV shows that provide the necessary shock our primal self calls for. Perhaps we have become so cosseted by the nanny state and mollycoddled as children that we have to look to irrational fears as a substitute for the rational fears our forbears felt. These irrational fears can then spread their tendrils far into our psyches, hijacking our imaginations and fuelled by sensationalist headlines in the media and online.

A more nature-connected and considered life can diminish the negative impacts of such unwanted irrational fears.

Write down an issue you have or a question you want answered. Then write below what you are doing about it or the answer as you see it. Take a moment to clear your mind and then write down the answer to the question, *'What would love do?'*

What is stopping you following this path of love?

With any issue, to coin a phrase from an online course facilitator, "Love on it."

Epilogue

Going deeper with shamanic healing

The exercises and practices shared in this book have some linkage and similarities with contemporary shamanic healing work, but to understand more or work on yourself at a deeper level, you need to work directly with a shamanic practitioner or similarly experienced spiritual worker.

Contemporary shamanic practitioners hold their healing sessions in a sacred and safe manner, creating a space for the client to understand themselves at a deeper level. The client is able to understand any current negative issues, see their true potential and release any blockages holding them back, while being fully supported and protected in the process.

The terminology for some of the healings and shamanic processes varies between practitioners. It is often rather poetic, mystical and spiritual in language, with labels such as *illumination, soul retrieval, past life clearing, contract breaking or entity extraction* commonly used.

However, the crucial part of any shamanic healing is the client's willingness to work with their life issues, traumas, painful experiences, illnesses or negative thought patterns. It is this readiness to move forward, and the intention that comes with it, that holds the true power. If a client is resistant to change, not wanting to be in the healing session or in denial of any potential benefits, it is unlikely they will gain any insight or feel an improvement – and, unfortunately, they could come away with an unfavourable view of the experience. Therefore, giving a shamanic practitioner at least two, ideally three sessions is prudent, so you become familiar with the process. As mentioned in the *exploring* exercise in *The East* section, when trying something new, there may be wariness and insecurity on the first attempt, understanding on the second and confidence thereafter. That said, if you have worked on yourself already, one session is often enough to make major breakthroughs.

In my shamanic healing sessions, the individual appointments are approximately one to one and a half hours. Each session typically involves an initial consultation where any questions can be answered before asking the client to lay on a therapy/massage couch where I conduct the contemporary shamanic work. I will normally use one or more objects from my spiritual altar, called a *mesa* (Spanish for table), the Q'ero term for a portable table of sacred objects (a medicine bundle), each of which has a specific healing purpose. The treatment often includes the gentle laying on of hands, the use of rattles, drums, voice or bells, and other shamanic tools to assist the process. [Some of the tools, including my mesa, are shown in the photo on the back cover of this book.] During the process, a variety of feelings, emotions or physical sensations can come up to be released. It is asked that the client be open to whatever happens and allow it to unfold, knowing they are in a safe, protected and loving space. This is a very loose outline, as the details will always depend upon the client's needs on the day.

Some sessions may be conducted outside, during a walk in nature, for example, where the connection to *Mother Earth* is palpable or even held remotely, as energy and intention are not limited by location, as the science of quantum entanglement is now beginning to shed light upon. (See *Father Sky* section.)

Shamanic healing can bring about significant emotional shifts. Sometimes years (or even lifetimes) of 'baggage' are surrendered nd transmuted, allowing the client to grow and move forward, feeling more authentic and in balance, and with a clearer understanding of their *soul* path. Personally, I believe shamanic healing sessions are effective for many issues, from physical ailments, emotional or mental imbalances, stress and anxiety, to personal development, spiritual connection and growth.

Shamanic healing is also just as powerful (sometimes more so) when working within a group. Drumming circles, healing shares, seasonal celebrations, fire ceremonies, group healings or specific courses and workshops all have their place, and offer chances for the individual to learn, heal and grow within a group setting. Such group work can be a direct link to ancestral celebrations and community togetherness, in addition to strengthening the connection to the Great Mystery and *what is*.

Final thoughts

Shamanism, and the other spiritual philosophies explored, have only been touched upon in these pages, but the connections and crossovers into other forms of spirituality and nature honouring are abundant in the modern world, as more and more people hear the call of *Mother Earth* and the life she supports. All manner of books, workshops, online tutorials and courses are available, so please seek out authentic practices and teachings that resonate with you. Remember, you are the result of evolution, a long line of ancestors behind you, over a kilometre long. Some traditions and practices have stuck, a number have been elaborated upon and a few have even become sacred or holy. However, over so many generations, many have also been distorted or lost. So, sometimes you must create your own. Find what feels right for you and trust your instincts.

It is my hope that within these pages, you have found some tools an techniques to help you navigate your life path more authentically and understand a little more about contemporary shamanism and the relationship we all have to life on this planet.

In *The South*, you worked with your past, discovering lessons from the events that have occurred during your life, finding healing where it was needed, and addressing any health issues you may have. *The West* moved you into, and through, your fears, learning to accept death as a part of life, and honouring any loved ones that have passed on. *The North* asked you to engage with your senses and connect with your inner child, to be more open to the wonder that exists in everyday life, while giving thanks to those that have been before. *The East* showed that maybe there is a bigger picture you may not be seeing, a calling based on your abilities, taking you closer to your dreams. *Mother Earth* helped strengthen your connection to the natural world, the elements and to all life on this planet. With *Father Sky*, you looked heavenward, beyond the Earth, and embraced the infinite and unimaginable, realising that you are part of the web of life, even if much is unknown to you. You have a right to be here. As such, you stand in the middle of your world, in *The Centre*, from where you were asked to find your own balance and decide how you wish to live in a truly authentic manner based on love, not fear.

However small you may feel at times, especially when compared to the eight billion other people on Earth, the enormity of the planet or the mind-boggling size of the known universe – a speck of dust, on a grain of sand, in an infinite sea – **you** are everything. **You** are king and queen, creator and destroyer. **You** are your own god or goddess and all-powerful in the kingdom of **you**. **You** can make a difference, not only to your own life but to the lives of others you share it with, be they human or animal. And for what purpose? Yes, to be the best u can, but also to share your gifts, to share your medicine, to help hers, and ultimately, be of service in the survival and proliferation f life on this incredible, sacred jewel of a planet we call home.

Be part of the solution, not part of the problem. Be open to and drive change. Be the change the world needs. Look to where your deepest longing meets the planet's greatest need, or as Frederick Buechner puts it, "The place God calls you to is the place where your deep gladness and the world's deep hunger meet."

I'll leave you with the poem I first encountered in my twenties while travelling, which has provided inspiration and comfort in equal measure ever since, Desiderata.

With much love
Trevor

Spring 2023

Desiderata
(latin "things desired"), published in 1925.

Go placidly amid the noise and haste and remember what peace there may be in silence.

As far as possible, without surrender, be on good terms with all persons. Speak your truth quietly and clearly and listen to others, even the dull and ignorant; they too have their story.

Avoid loud and aggressive persons, they are a vexation to the spirit.

If you compare yourself to others, you may become vain and bitter; for always there will be greater and lesser persons than yourself.

Enjoy your achievements as well as your plans.

Keep interested in your own career, however humble; it is a real possession in the changing fortunes of time.

Exercise caution in your business affairs; for the world is full of trickery, but let this not blind you to what virtue there is; many persons strive for high ideals, and everywhere life is full of heroism.

Be yourself.

Especially, do not feign affection.

Neither be cynical about love; for in the face of all aridity and disenchantment, it is perennial as the grass.

Take kindly the counsel of the years, gracefully surrendering the things of youth.

Nurture strength of spirit to shield you in sudden misfortune, but do not distress yourself with imaginings. Many fears are born of fatigue and loneliness.

Beyond a wholesome discipline, be gentle with yourself.

You are a child of the Universe, no less than the trees and the stars; you have a right to be here, and whether or not it is clear to you, no doubt the Universe is unfolding as it should.

Therefore be at peace with God, whatever you conceive God to be, and whatever your labours and aspirations.

In the noisy confusion of life, keep peace with your soul.

With all its sham, drudgery and broken dreams, it is still a beautiful world.

Be careful.

Strive to be happy.

Max Ehrmann (1872-1945)

Acknowledgements

Thanks firstly must go to those that have gone before, and to the indigenous peoples worldwide who keep the old ways alive and are willing to share their knowledge and wisdom, with a special thank you to the Q'eros of the Peruvian highlands.

Thank you to my teacher, Skie Hummingbird, for her guidance, support and humour over the many years And to her husband, Red, and the numerous others met, shared with, and learnt from within the Sungate family while training, on a course or just popping round for a cuppa. And talking of the odd cuppa, cheers Matt Keane for sharing so much and always having the kettle on.

Thank you to the individuals, groups and societies that champion mother nature and honouring the indigenous ways, and who have helped me on my path, such as Nicholas Breeze Wood & Faith Nolton with their quarterly magazine Sacred Hoop, The Way of the Buzzard, The Sacred Trust, Embercombe, The Animas Valley Institute and Peace Retreat to name just a few.

To all the shamanic practitioners, spiritual healers and energy workers out there trying to make a difference. I salute you.

Much gratitude goes to all the holders of drum circles, healing shares and seasonal celebrations, especially to Jo Gray and Pete Wardle for their joy of drumming, endless enthusiasm, and for helping me birth my own hand drum many years ago.

For help putting this book together, thank you to Mark Dowding and Helen Fram for their editing advice. And for the inspiration to go it alone, thank you Sue Stone. However, self-publishing (and self-editing) does mean all the mistakes, grammatical errors and poor English are on me. So apologies for any you find.

Finally, a huge thank you to my friends and family, especially to mum in spirit, Margaret and Dad, and Alison, Simon, Ruby and Anna for all their love, support and understanding.

Printed in Great Britain
by Amazon

23762225R00158